Mu

A Sho

ost biographies tell you what an individual did followed by what he did next. This biography does much more. In addition to recounting the story of Muhammad's life, it assesses his importance in Islam right up to the present, particularly in such topical issues as *jihad*, apostasy, the status of women, the Salman Rushdie affair and interfaith relationships.

Views of Muhammad's life often polarize Muslims and others and most biographies about Muhammad are no exception – Western biographies emphasize the military, assessing Muhammad's actions in twentieth-century terms; Muslim ones emphasize the spiritual. But in this study, Martin Forward has no axe to grind; he explores Muhammad's actions in the context of his society, producing a balanced and readable presentation from which readers can draw their own conclusions.

Martin Forward has taught Islam at the universities of Leicester, Bristol and Cambridge. He is currently Senior Tutor and Lecturer in Pastoral and Systematic Theology, Wesley House, Cambridge and is a member of the Cambridge University Faculty of Divinity. He is ordained in the Methodist Church and has a life-long fascination with Islam.

Other books in this series:

A Short History of the Bahá'í Faith, Peter Smith, ISBN 1-85168-070-5

A Short History of Buddhism, Edward Conze, ISBN 1-85168-066-7

A Short History of Islam, William Montgomery Watt, ISBN 1-85168-109-4

A Short History of Judaism, Lavinia and Dan Cohn-Sherbok, ISBN 1-85168-069-1

A Short Introduction to the Bahá'í Faith, Moojan Momen, ISBN 1-85168-120-5

A Short Introduction to Islamic Philosophy, Theology and Mysticism, Majid Fakhry, ISBN 1-85168-134-5

A Short Introduction to Judaism, Lavinia and Dan Cohn-Sherbok, ISBN 1-85168-145-0

A Short Introduction to the Old Testament Prophets, E. W. Heaton, ISBN 1-85168-114-0

A Short Reader in Judaism, Lavinia and Dan Cohn-Sherbok, ISBN 1-85168-112-4

Other books on Islamic Studies published by Oneworld:

City of Wrong: A Friday in Jerusalem, M. Kamel Hussein (trans. Kenneth Cragg), ISBN 1-85168-072-1

Companion to the Qur'án, William Montgomery Watt, ISBN 1-85168-036-5

Defenders of Reason in Islam: Mu'tazilism from Medieval School to Modern Symbol, ISBN 1-85168-147-7

The Event of the Qur'án: Islam in its Scripture, Kenneth Cragg, ISBN 1-85168-067-5

The Faith and Practice of Al-Ghazálí, William Montgomery Watt, ISBN 1-85168-062-4

Islam and the West, Norman Daniel, ISBN 1-85168-129-9

Jesus in the Qur'án, Geoffrey Parrinder, ISBN 1-85168-094-2

Muslims and Christians Face to Face, Kate Zebiri, ISBN 1-85168-133-7

Muslim Devotions: A Study of Prayer-Manuals in Common Use, Constance E. Padwick, ISBN 1-85168-115-9

On Being a Muslim: Finding a Religious Path in the World Today, Farid Esack, ISBN 1-85168-146-9

The Qur'án and its Exegesis: Selected Texts with Classical and Modern Muslim Interpretations, Helmut Gätje, ISBN 1-85168-118-3

Qur'án, Liberation and Pluralism, Farid Esack, ISBN 1-85168-121-3

Rabi'a: The Life and Work of Rabi'a and Other Women Mystics in Islam, Margaret Smith, ISBN 1-85168-085-3

Rúmí: Poet and Mystic, Reynold A. Nicholson, ISBN 1-85168-096-9

Voices of Islam, John Bowker, ISBN 1-85168-095-0

Muhammad:
A Short Biography

Martin Forward

ONEWORLD
OXFORD

MUHAMMAD: A SHORT BIOGRAPHY

Oneworld Publications
(Sales and Editorial)
185 Banbury Road
Oxford OX2 7AR
England

Oneworld Publications
(US Marketing Office)
PO Box 830, 21 Broadway
Rockport, MA 01966
USA

ISBN 1-85168-131-0

Cover design by Peter Maguire
Printed and bound by WSOY, Finland

Contents

Acknowledgements   vii

Introduction   1
Perspectives   1
Sources   2
Intention   3

Map: West Asia at the time of Muhammad   6

1 The Prophet of Islam   7
The Makings of a Prophet   8
The Prophet in Makka   11
The Emigration to Madina   15
The Prophet Triumphant   28

2 Muhammad and the Unity of God   31
The Seal of the Prophets   31
The Status and Integrity of the Quran   33

The Sources of Sunni Islam   37
An Alternative Way: Shia Islam   40
Mystic Paths   42
Muhammad in Popular Islam   49

3 Muhammad and Other World Faiths   54

Muhammad, Jews and Christians   54
Muhammad: Defender of the Faith   59
Muhammad and Jesus   66
Islam: A Minority Religion   72

4 Muhammad and the Role of Women   77

The Quran, the Sharia and Women   78
Muhammad's Marriages   83
Muslim Women in the Contemporary World   94

5 Muhammad in Recent Debate   98

Muhammad and Radical Western Scholars   98
Muhammad and the Orientalists   102
Muhammad and Christians   105
Muhammad and the Unbelievers   108
History and Myth   110
Muhammad in Muslim Estimation   116
Muhammad: A Personal Estimate   119

Glossary   121

Bibliography   123

Further Reading   126

Index   128

Acknowledgements

I alone am responsible for what I have written. But I owe a debt to countless friends. Those who taught me Islam, especially John Bowker, Alan Macleod, and Peter Hardy, inculcated in me a respect for the disciplined religious imagination. They also commended and commanded a rigorous search for historical and theological truth. My two years as a fraternal worker at the Henry Martyn Institute of Islamic Studies, Hyderabad, India, from 1975 to 1977 were a formative influence upon me. I remember with affection my colleagues there, especially David Lindell and Andreas D'Souza; and my Arabic teacher, Hayath Khan, who taught me a great deal about the spirituality of Islam. I owe much to Ursula King in understanding the contemporary debates in Religious Studies. Among others Eric Lott, Kenneth Cracknell, David Craig and Mohammed Alam have been particularly inspirational.

Although my period of specialization is in the field of South Asian modernist Islam, I have long been intrigued by Islam's central human figure. I am grateful to Novin Doostdar and Juliet Mabey of Oneworld Publications for allowing me the opportunity of writing this life of the Prophet of Islam, and to them and their colleagues at Oneworld, particularly Helen Coward, for the intricacies of bringing this work to birth. Novin's careful comments about the original manuscript have been invaluable. I am also thankful to Dr Khazeh Fananapazir for a number of helpful suggestions.

I am indebted to countless previous biographers of Muhammad, peace be upon him, and to many books, articles and conversations. I no longer have any clear idea of the origin of many of the views that I have formed about him. I am grateful to my sources. I apologize if I have misrepresented them, and for failing to acknowledge their influence in precise detail. Despite these debts, I alone am responsible for what I have written.

Long years after I was involved with and in the world of Islam, my late father told me how he had nearly become a Muslim when he served in Hadhramaut during and after the Second World War. He had been deeply impressed by the religious life of Arab and Indian Muslims with whom he worked. I remember him with admiration, gratitude and affection.

I dedicate this book to Udho, my wife, and Naomi, my daughter.

Introduction

Perspectives

There are many books about Muhammad, some for the specialist and others for the general reader. They are written from a variety of perspectives and reveal as much about their authors as their subject, so it seems reasonable to reveal my own viewpoint, as far as I can.

I am not a Muslim, but a Christian. For part of my childhood I lived in Aden, at the heel of the Arabian peninsula. I made several Muslim friends there, and Islam began to exercise a fascination for me that has never ceased. The faith and devotion of Muslims excite my curiosity and admiration. I am not among those who study the faith of Islam to condemn it and its Prophet, though I have never considered abandoning the Christian religion.

I write first and foremost out of more than thirty years of relationships, including strong friendships, with Muslims. Friendship bestows privileges. With my Muslim friends, I have been able to raise contentious and divisive issues between their religion and my own. Mutual esteem and humour have diffused any tension. Friendship also imparts the obligation to write charitably and respectfully, especially about the heart of religion, which is where Muhammad is located for Muslims.

I agree with my revered mentor and friend, Geoffrey Parrinder, a founder of the modern discipline of Religious Studies, that it is often faith that best understands faith. This is not to deny the many insights revealed by atheist and agnostic biographers of Muhammad. It is to question the secular sacred cow that objectivity (a slippery word when it comes to the great issues of life and death with which religions deal) is only possible to those who are not committed to the issues with which they deal. This is as odd as suggesting that the study of mathematics can only adequately be undertaken by someone who questions its point and value. I have tried to write honestly, from my own particular religious but Christian perspective. I have borne in mind the evocative words of W. B. Yeats, from his poem 'He wishes for the Cloths of Heaven':

> I have spread my dreams under your feet;
> Tread softly because you tread on my dreams.

However, precisely because I am not a Muslim, I offer a standpoint upon the importance of the great Arabian Prophet different from that of Muslims. Certainly, I would not claim it to be a better one. Rather, I suggest that it is through the various portraits of Muhammad offered by several viewpoints that the meaning and influence of this significant man of God emerge with compelling power for many more people than Muslims alone.

Because my experiential knowledge of Muslims has gone hand in hand with an academic interest in Islam, I know well the difficulties attending the enterprise of a Christian biography of Muhammad. For reasons that will become clear (see chapter 3), relations between Christians and Muslims have often been profoundly distrustful, even destructive. Both groups are suspicious of what the other writes of them and their religion. Yet neither can be overprotective of their prophets and beliefs, since both claim them to be mercy for humankind, not tribal possessions forbidden to others. At any rate, I write from faith, about the Prophet of another faith, and recognize that great issues of universal truth and dialogue are raised by such an enterprise.

Sources

A word about the title of this book, *Muhammad: A Short Biography*. In my view (with which most Muslims would disagree), it is as difficult to write a biography of Muhammad as it is of any other historical religious founder, such as the Buddha and Jesus. Like their lives, Muhammad's is filtered to us through the confessional beliefs of devotees. The major sources for a life of Muhammad are the Quran and the *hadith*. The Quran (or 'recitation') is, in Muslim belief, the uncreated word of God revealed through Jibril (Gabriel) to the prophet Muhammad. The traditional Muslim understanding is that the Quran was finally collected together when Uthman was caliph, less than twenty years after the Prophet's death. A *hadith* (plural *ahadith*) is an oral tradition that describes a deed or saying of the Prophet. As such, it is a source of Islamic law second in importance only to the Quran (see chapter 2, pp. 37–9). The standard Muslim biography of Muhammad is Ibn Hisham's (d. 833 or 828) revision of Ibn Ishaq's (d. *c.*767) work. Another important early scholar is Tabari (*c.*839–923), a historian and quranic exegete.

Muslims and Western scholars have interpreted the information these and other early sources yield, very differently. Yet until recently, with some exceptions, a scholarly consensus of Muslims and non-Muslims alike accepted their basic reliability as a means of accessing the historical Muhammad. Within the last twenty years, this consensus has broken down. A generation of Western scholars has come to question their value as sources for constructing a biography of the Prophet, and counts them as confessional, sectarian creations.

I have adopted a conservative, traditional approach to them, but raise the issue head on in chapter 5.

Intention

There is another reason for not resting content with a straightforward account of Muhammad's life, which has little to do with a recognition that it is difficult to piece that life together from the written and other materials that are available to us. This second, very important reason judges that a bare account of the life of Muhammad is only the beginning of recognizing his importance for Muslims, indeed for all humankind. He has guided the actions and thoughts of Muslims, to the point where many justify their deeds and words on the basis that his words and deeds sanction theirs.

There are particular issues that exercise contemporary scholars of Religious Studies, to which Muhammad has made a contribution, either because the sources suggest that he spoke about or at least alluded to them, or else because Muslims have constructed or justified their beliefs about them with reference to him. Many of these issues are raised nowadays in the light of the fact that the modern world is a much more interconnected place than it was. Among them are: what is the meaning and end of religious systems? What should be the role of women in religions at the end of the second millennium of the Common Era? How does transcendent reality impinge itself upon this world of sensory perception and rational discourse, and what does it require of us? And what is the place of myth and history in understanding the truths religions aspire to reveal and structure?

My intention has been to write about Muhammad's importance to such questions, for Muslims and for sympathetic outsiders. I am less interested in recounting what he did and what he did next (even supposing that to be a reasonable pursuit, as I do to a point), than in demonstrating how he has been deemed important by various groups of Muslims, and by non-Muslims as well.

In my opinion, the genius of Islam has been to enshrine the ideal of a single human community in which political, social and economic matters are held together as the will of the one God for humankind. So chapter 1 outlines the life of the Prophet Muhammad, to illustrate this central aspect of God's message through him. Chapter 2 asks how far this ideal has been achieved in Islamic history and whether it remains, or ever was, a realistic or even desirable goal. Chapter 3 interrogates Islam's attitude towards other communities of faith, which pursue different, perhaps irreconcilable, goals for human beings. Chapter 4 examines Islam's teaching about the status of men and women. Chapter 5 briefly explores current research on Islamic origins and assesses the measure of Muhammad for Muslims and non-Muslims.

My aim has been to write a non-technical book. To that end I decided to do away altogether with the apparatus of diacritical marks in transliterating Arabic words, even when I have quoted from other works where they are included. These tools merely baffle the non-professional. However, I have attempted to make the transliterations as exact as possible: hence, for example, Quran, not Qur'án or the incorrect but common Koran. I have often consulted Ian Netton's invaluable *A Popular Dictionary of Islam* (London, Curzon Press, 1992) to check his spellings of English transliterations of Arabic words, and have usually followed his lead, except that he includes diacritical marks. In some places I have approached pedantry, as in preferring Makka and Madina to Mecca and Medina. So be it: flawlessness is not possible in this area. I have followed Common Era datings, rather than giving dates from the Muslim calendar (AH, *Anno Hegirae*, 'from the year of the *hijra*', the date of Muhammad's emigration from Makka to Madina in CE 622, when the Muslim calendar begins).

There are many translations into English of the divine word vouchsafed to Muhammad in the Arabic tongue. Most are either too reverential (perhaps in imitation of the Authorized Version of the Bible), or dull, or unhelpfully obscure, or very often a combination of all these. So I have provided my own renderings of quranic passages. Sometimes, I have run the risk of offering approximate rather than accurate translations. At least the inelegant interpretations or mistakes or ambiguities are my own.

When Muslims mention Muhammad or another Muslim prophet in speech or print, they usually follow the name with an expression in Arabic which can be translated, 'May God bless him and grant him salvation.' The fact that usually I do not implies no discourtesy but simply follows academic convention in Western scholarship. I have learned much in researching and writing this book, and my admiration for Muhammad has not diminished. The time has surely come for a growing number of non-Muslim monotheists to grapple with the issue of how, if at all, God has used Muhammad as a mercy for humankind. I raise this issue in chapter 3, and then, more personally, at the end of this book in chapter 5.

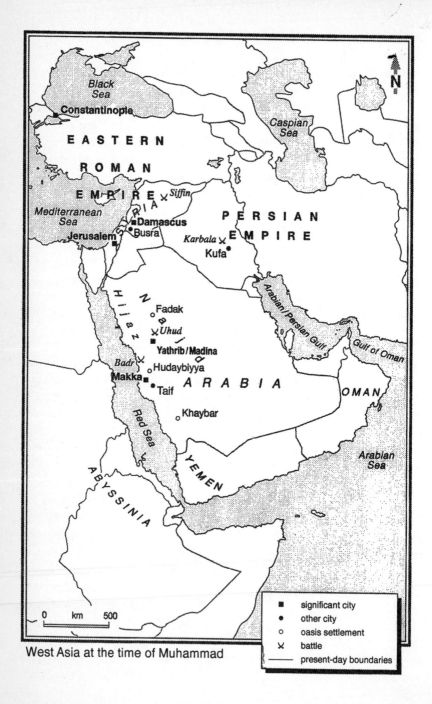

West Asia at the time of Muhammad

The Prophet of Islam

On 8 June 632, the Prophet Muhammad died with his head on the breast of his favourite living wife, Aisha. Within the previous two years, he had become master of most of the Arabian peninsula. For over twenty years he had received, at irregular but frequent intervals, revelations from the one God, who has no partners or equals.

That monotheistic vision had created a community of faithful believers, obedient to God's Prophet and the divine words he uttered. The question was whether Islam ('submission [to God]', by extension, 'peace') would survive his death and, if so, how. Some of Muhammad's earliest followers, including Umar, who was to be his second successor (*khalifa*) as political head of the Muslim community, refused to believe he had passed away. It was an even older disciple, Abu Bakr, soon to become the first *khalifa*, who comforted and put courage into Umar. Then the older man addressed the distraught crowd: 'Men, those who worshipped Muhammad must know that Muhammad is dead. But for those who worship God, God lives and will never die'. Then he quoted a quranic verse as proof: 'Muhammad is nothing more than a Messenger. Many have been the messengers who died before him. If he died or were slain, would you then turn back upon your heels?' (Q3.144). Then the crowd accepted the death of Muhammad, Prophet of God.

Yet, in death, Muhammad lives on as the human founder of Islam. This chapter explores his central importance in the creation of that community (*umma*).

The Makings *of a* Prophet

Muhammad was born in Makka about the year 570. This town is located in Arabia, a large, arid peninsula in West Asia about 1300 miles long and 750 wide, which is mainly desert with a few oases (see map, p. 6). Islam's holy scripture, the Quran, describes Makka as situated 'in an uncultivated valley' (Q14.37). Specifically, it is in the Hijaz (from the Arabic *hijaz*, 'barrier'), the mountain range between the western coast and the desert plateau of Najd. There, the summers are hot. Rain falls irregularly in the winter, sometimes in heavy storms, and long periods of drought are not unknown.

The geography of Arabia was an important factor in Muhammad's career. The climate prevented an agricultural base so it was not a wealthy area. However, it was, by the time of Muhammad, comparatively homogeneous, consisting mainly of Arabs who spoke a single language, Arabic. Many of these Arabs were nomads whose way of life contributed to the uniformity of Arab civilization. They travelled widely after whatever sustenance was to be had, mostly cattle-breeding, hunting and a little trading. They also robbed caravans and settlements in raids, except during three months (the seventh, eleventh and twelfth of the lunar year). Then, it was forbidden by religious sanction.

Many scholars argue that Makka was, by the standards of its time and location, a thriving market town, on trade routes to India, Africa and Persia. Recent research has strongly questioned this presupposition (see chapter 5, p. 101). Certainly, Makka, though often called a city by biographers of Muhammad, had none of the trappings of great economic success: its dwellings were huts made of palm branches clustered around a spring and a cube-shaped stone house, the sanctuary of a god or gods. Its name may derive from the Sabaean word *mukarrib* (sanctuary), which could refer to its sacred shrine, the Kaba.

Its inhabitants had until recently been bedouins. Five generations before Muhammad, his ancestor, Qusayy, obtained possession of

Makka. He settled there with his fellow-tribesmen, the Quraysh.[1]

Qusayy's grandson, Hashim, Muhammad's great-grandfather, established the Quraysh as merchants of standing, by negotiating rights and protection with the rulers of Byzantium, Persia, Ethiopia and Yemen. Some Western writers have argued that in their transformation from cattle breeders to merchants, the Makkans had become oppressive capitalists, but any interpretation of Muhammad as a prototype Marxist begs more questions than it solves. However alluring such a view has been throughout much of the twentieth century, it looks distinctly anachronistic now.

Muhammad was born to Abdallah and Amina, of the clan of Hashim in the tribe of Quraysh. His father died before he was born, and his mother when he was six years old. He was then looked after by his paternal grandfather, Abd al-Muttalib, who died two years later. Thereafter, his paternal uncle, Abu Talib, brought him up to manhood. Despite the sentimental interpretations of some biographers, this is not a sad tale of an orphaned and unloved boy. Muhammad's cannot have been a very unusual case in the rigours of sixth-century Arabia. Moreover, his childhood in the environment of an extended family shows that not all networks of social care had been abandoned in the drive by Makkans for economic betterment. Indeed, Abu Talib is reported to have cared for him so much that he rarely let the boy out of his sight.

Early accounts of the life of Muhammad suggest that his ministry was foretold by Christian monks, Jewish rabbis and Arab soothsayers. Some Ethiopian Christians told his foster-mother that they wanted to take him to their king, foreseeing a glorious future for him. Earlier still, when his mother had been pregnant with him, a light came from her which illuminated the castles of Busra in Syria. Later, when Muhammad was a young boy, he and Abu Talib went there in a merchant caravan. A monk in Busra, called Bahira, told Abu Talib of the boy's importance, and warned him to guard Muhammad against the Jews.

Little is known of Muhammad's boyhood, adolescence and early manhood. He is described as shy and reserved, though relaxed among his friends. He was simple in habits of food and dress, and fond of children. Before Muhammad received revelations from God, the Quraysh called him 'the trustworthy one'. This designation dates from the rebuilding of the Kaba when he was thirty-five years old. A dispute had arisen between different clans of the Quraysh about who should

1. The different groupings in seventh-century Arabia were various and complex. I use the word 'tribe' to describe larger groupings, and 'clan' to describe smaller ones. For a helpful discussion, consult Watt, *Muhammad at Medina*, chapters 4 and 5.

have the privilege of placing the sacred black stone in the renovated building. Muhammad was asked to intervene and found a tactful solution: he placed the stone on a cloak and different clan representatives each held an end and carried it to its appointed place.

A wealthy Makkan woman, Khadija, heard of Muhammad's sterling qualities. She engaged him to run her deceased husband's business. They married when he was twenty-five and she forty. Seven children were born to them. The three boys died. One daughter, Fatima, was to become extremely important in the teachings and devotions of Shia Islam (see chapter 2, pp. 40–2).

Unlike many Arabs of his day Muhammad was a religious man and would often retire to a cave in Mount Hira, three miles north of Makka. There he would pray. He disapproved of what he saw as the inadequacies of his contemporaries' religion. He forsook idolatry and worshipped Allah, the one God. (Allah comes from *al-Ilah*, which means 'The God'.) The conviction grew in him that God would judge all people, offering hellfire for the wicked and paradise for the obedient.

Muslims call pre-Islamic Arabia, *al-jahiliyya*. This term, found four times in the Quran in allusion to the concept itself, is usually translated as 'the age of ignorance'. This ignorance (or even savagery) derived, so Muslims believe, from the widespread polytheism of that time, which meant that pagans were ignorant of God. However, the name of Muhammad's father (Abd Allah means 'servant of the one God') shows that there was some belief in a controlling or supreme God. Makkans held that Allah had three daughters, al-Lat (the mother goddess, consort of the moon), al-Uzza (possibly the patron goddess of Makka) and Manat (the goddess of fate and death). These daughters were, in the practice of most Makkans, more important then their father, who seems to have been a distant, though benign, supreme being. It was the achievement of Islam, which means 'peace', to transform Arabia and lands far beyond, from ignorance to the harmony that comes from knowing the unity of God.

Muhammad was not a lone figure. He seems to have been one of a number of people who, just before the coming of Islam, sought a more pure and challenging form of religion than the pervasive polytheism. Muslim scholars record that there were people contemporary with Muhammad and before his time called *hunafa* (the plural of *hanif*). These were followers of the religion of Abraham. According to the

Quran (3.67), Abraham was neither a Jew nor a Christian but a *hanif*, a *muslim*, and not among the idolaters. The word *hanif* in pre-Islamic poetry could mean a pagan or idol worshipper. The Quran, however, gives to it the completely different meaning of monotheist. It was Muhammad's particular achievement to establish the one God Allah's crucial and sole importance for Arabs and, indeed, all creation.

About the year 610 when Muhammad was in the cave on Mount Hira, he received a revelation. The angel Gabriel (in Arabic, Jibril) brought him the command of God. He ordered Muhammad to recite and pressed down so tightly on him with a coverlet of brocade that Muhammad thought he would die. There was writing on the coverlet. The words he was given are Q96.1–5:

> Recite in the name of the Lord who created, created humans from clots of blood. Recite, for your Lord is merciful. He has taught the use of the pen, taught humans what they do not know.

Muhammad thought, to his dismay, that he was either a poet or one possessed, or else would be rejected as such by his kith and kin. He returned to Khadija, confused and terrified. She told her husband that God would not mislead him, an honourable man, and expressed her hope that he would be the Prophet of his people. She consulted her cousin Waraqa, who had become a Christian. He declared that Muhammad had received the message that had come to Moses and Jesus, and would be the Arabs' Prophet.

According to some Muslim sources, a gap of six months followed this first experience (though others say up to three years), during which Muhammad received no more prophecies. Then a voice came with the words 'You, wrapped in your cloak. Arise and be a warner. Praise your Lord. Purify your clothing. Flee the wrath' (Q74.1–5). (Some sources give Q96.1–5 as the first revelation, others Q74.1–5 or 1–7. Yet others conflate the accounts as I have done.)

The Prophet *in* Makka

After this experience, Muhammad assumed his role as Prophet. Prophecy came to him, piecemeal and through the mediation of Jibril, until his death in 632. His first followers were members of his immediate family: his wife Khadija; his cousin Ali; and Zayd ibn

Haritha, a freed slave who remained in his household as his adopted son. Abu Bakr, who became the first caliph, also followed him. Then others gradually joined. Within about three years, there were some fifty Makkans who were Muslims, which means 'those who submit [to God]'. These earliest followers were won by private preaching, but thereafter Muhammad began to proclaim his message publicly.

His earliest message was against idolatry. He warned his listeners that God is one, the only creator, the judge who will call humans to account on the last day. Then, the good will inherit paradise and the wicked burn in hellfire (Q92). Idolatry is particularly reprehensible: 'Say: He is God, the one, eternal. He has no offspring and was not born. No one can be compared to him' (Q112). These words were eventually used against Christian Trinitarianism, and even imperfect Jewish adherence to monotheism (Q9.30). But at first, God's word was addressed to the pagan Makkans.

This emphasis upon the unity of God was not a new message in the religious history of humankind. Muhammad was conscious that he stood in a line of prophets, from Adam to Jesus. But at this early stage of his ministry, his message was primarily local, not universal. He referred to the revelation as an 'Arabic Quran':

> We [God] have revealed to you an Arabic Quran, so that you may warn the mother of cities [i.e. Makka], and all around it; and warn her of the day of which there is no doubt when all will be assembled, and some will be in paradise and others in hell. (Q42.7)

Once, when Satan composed verses which Muhammad mistakenly believed had come from God, the Prophet seemed to waver in his commitment to a strict monotheism (see chapter 2, pp. 34–5). Yet this vacillation was only momentary.

The unity of God has always been central to Islam and seems to have been so from its beginnings. When Muslims profess their faith, they make the act of *tashahhud*, 'giving one's testimony'. Normally this is in the form of the *kalima* (word) that 'there is no god but God, and Muhammad is the Prophet of God'. This profession does not occur as such in the Quran, but its elements occur in several places. The *kalima* is used often, not least at life's profoundest moments, on the occasions of births, deaths, and praying. Later Islamic scholars came to believe that it must be perfectly understood, believed in the heart and pronounced without hesitation. Such refinements came into being after

Muhammad's death, but they show how central monotheism was to his teaching. It was wholly contrary to the pagan religion of the Arabs it replaced.

The Quran told the Makkans that, to escape hell, they should cease to worship idols, in the Kaba and elsewhere. These were lifeless things, unable to help themselves or others (Q7.191–5), and flimsy as cobwebs (Q29.41). This attack upon local deities deeply offended many Makkans. Partly, it was to do with the reverence in which people hold their superstitions. Also, no doubt some Makkans made money when people came to the Kaba during the sacred months. They did not wish to see the source of their wealth undermined by new religious teachings.

It was the apparent absurdity of the new teachings that most struck them. Most pagan Arabs believed neither in heaven nor hell. To be sure, religion had important ritualistic and other functions in this life. When people wanted to propitiate the gods they might consult clairvoyants or other seers who glimpsed the supernatural world, or they might confer with the *jinn* (intelligent, usually invisible beings made from flame, some, but not all of whom obey God), hobgoblins and other mischievous or malevolent beings. However, at death, humans ceased to exist. The Quran depicts Makkans saying: 'There is only our life on this earth, and we shall never be raised again' (Q6.29).

At first, Muhammad's teaching seemed to his opponents to be foolish, impious and irrelevant. Some Makkans were willing to pay for Muhammad to be exorcized, if he gave up or modified his religion. Others would even make him king (so some sources say, though this seems less likely, unless they were speaking in mockery). Then, as some followed him, including young people, it also came to appear potentially dangerous. Those who believed and acted upon his words elevated him to a powerful position, for in claiming him as a messenger or a prophet, the Quran implicitly demanded obedience to him as the mouthpiece of God.

The portions of the Quran revealed to Muhammad in Makka contain stories of messengers whose message had been rejected by their people, but who were eventually vindicated by God. Like Muhammad, they preached the unity of God and the certainty of judgement, but were ignored or derided by most of their hearers. Many were figures drawn from Judaeo–Christian sacred history. One was Musa (or Moses), who was sent as a warner to Pharaoh (Q79.15–26).

Messengers were drawn from many cultures. Salih was an Arab whom God sent to the tribe of Thamud. Its members spurned his warnings and cut off the feet of his she-camel, which had been given them as a sign of God's mercy. God's wrath at the impious actions of this tribe led to their destruction (Q91.11–15; cf. Q7.73–9).

The new religion laid bare deep clan divisions among the Quraysh. Most of Muhammad's earliest followers came from his own descent group from Qusayy, the Banu Hashim, yet not all of them acknowledged him as a prophet and some Arabs from other groups did. The new religion was weakest among the Banu Abd Shams, the fiercest rivals of the Banu Hashim. It was not in the Banu Abd Shams' interest to support the religious claims of a member of another clan. If widely accepted, these claims would give Muhammad social and religious prestige and power, so they led a boycott of Muhammad's descent group.

The Arabs were protected and chastised by the clan to which they belonged. Then, there was no strong religion to provide sanctions against antisocial behaviour, as Islam was soon to do. Any insult or threat to a clan member from outsiders would result in the rest of the clan springing to his or her defence. There would be reprisals, either against the perpetrators or others from their clan. Inter-clan feuds were common, but often were controlled by mediators who pressed for a negotiated settlement. Any unruly clansman could have his group's protection withdrawn, a terrible punishment, since he could then be punished or killed with impunity.

Muhammad himself was safe from Makkan persecution. His uncle, Abu Talib, was powerful enough to offer him protection. Other Muslims were not so fortunate. Several believers were imprisoned, or beaten, or allowed no food and drink. Some gave way and recanted their faith, but others did not. Bilal, an Abyssinian slave, was regularly brought out in the hottest part of the day. He was spread-eagled on his back, and a great rock was put on his chest. He was told to deny Muhammad and worship al-Lat and al-Uzza, but refused, murmuring, 'One, one.' Eventually, Abu Bakr bought him in exchange for a stronger, heathen slave. He freed Bilal, who became the first *muadhdhin* (muezzin), the person who gives the call to prayer from the minaret of a mosque. Such incidents illustrate the egalitarian implications of Islam: all believers, even slaves of another race, are brothers and sisters.

Members of the new religion needed space to become a kind of clan against other groups, or to form a company of believers whose loyalty transcended clan obligations. Until then, they would be vulnerable to persecution or even death. So, in 615 Muhammad let fifteen Muslims emigrate to Abyssinia, where they were protected by the Christian ruler. Others joined them there later, and eventually they numbered about eighty men and twenty women in all.

In Makka, the religion gained notable converts, despite harassment. In 616, the warrior Hamza struck a particular enemy of Muhammad called Amr (known by Muslims as Abu Jahl, which means 'the father of ignorance') for abusing the Prophet, and claimed 'I follow his religion.' Later, Umar bin al-Khattab, who had set out to kill Muhammad, was moved by his teaching and became a Muslim, to the amazement of the Makkans. Eventually, Umar became the second caliph.

The Emigration *to* Madina

In 619, Muhammad's precarious position became downright perilous. Khadija and Abu Talib died. The former had provided financial security, love and reassurance; the latter, protection from his Makkan enemies. Abu Lahab succeeded his brother, Abu Talib, as chief of the Banu Hashim. The Banu Hashim had suffered from the persecution against Muhammad and the boycott other clans had placed on them: other groups had refused intermarriage or commercial dealings with them until they put a stop to Muhammad's preaching. At first, Abu Lahab extended protection to his nephew, but he later withdrew it. His outward reason for withdrawing protection was that, after questioning, Muhammad admitted that Abd al-Muttalib, the Prophet's pagan grandfather, was in hell. Because of these offensive remarks about their common ancestor, Abu Lahab could withdraw protection without losing face or honour. His name means 'the father of flame'. He was so called, some sources say, because of his fiery temper and ruddy complexion. The Quran plays on this appellation to condemn him and his wife to hellfire (Q111).

This incident illustrates Muhammad's deep commitment to the worship of Allah, the one God. Abd al-Muttalib had taken care of Muhammad after his mother died, yet the logic of quranic monotheism is that heathen practices are not acceptable from anyone, not even from the relatives of prophets. To this extent, Muhammad was like Abraham, who condemned even his own father for idol worship (Q46.23ff.). This deeply offended Arabs, who reverenced the memory of their ancestors. Non-Muslims sometimes judge Muhammad very harshly for his lack of family piety. They should hesitate before doing so. The sources do not suggest that Muhammad gloried in condemning his relatives; somewhat the opposite, in fact. Rather, his controlling vision was that the greater good of humankind is wrought by acknowledging, worshipping and obeying the one God. All personal opinions and affections should be subordinate to the transforming power of monotheism.

At first, after his rejection by Abu Lahab, Muhammad contemplated a move to Taif, a town about seventy miles from Makka. But the content of his preaching won him no friends there, and he was stoned. He returned to Makka, where he spoke at local fairs to some nomadic tribes, but again met with no success.

Then an opportunity opened for him in Yathrib, a prosperous town around two hundred and fifty miles to the north of Makka, about a week's journey on foot. A group of six men came from there in 620, on pilgrimage to the Kaba (hajj). They listened with interest to the Prophet's message of peace (islam), pledged loyalty to Muhammad, and accepted him as Prophet. This is called the 'first pledge of Aqaba', after the area near Makka where they met. The following year, a small group of twelve (including five of the original six) came back. The next year, 622, a more important group of seventy-three men and two women interviewed Muhammad during the festival of the hajj. An agreement was made on this last occasion, the 'second pledge of Aqaba'. The group from Yathrib took an oath to obey Muhammad and to fight for him. An uncle of Muhammad, al-Abbas, was present to see that the Prophet's protection was now the responsibility of his allies in Yathrib. (It may be that the sources have conflated one crucial meeting into several.)

Why did some inhabitants of Yathrib want Muhammad to go there? Unlike the citizens of Makka, who formed a relatively homogeneous population, most of whom were members of a single tribe, the Quraysh, Yathrib had been settled by disparate groups. The tribes of the Aws and the Khazraj were particularly suspicious of each other and jostled for control over rights to land and water. There were also many Jews. Three main clans (out of perhaps eleven in all) followed the

Jewish religion: al-Nadir, Qurayza and Qaynuqa. It is uncertain whether they were descended from Jews or from Arab families which had embraced Judaism. They had intermarried with Arab tribes, from whom there may have been little to distinguish them, except for religious beliefs and practices. However, some scholars argue that the Jews, who were engaged mainly in agriculture and handicrafts, were culturally and economically superior to the Arabs, most of whom disliked them.

There had been much strife between different clans in Yathrib, culminating at the Battle of Buath, which occurred about 618. In pre-Islamic Arabia, certain men were regarded as wise enough to arbitrate in such disputes. Muhammad was a neutral figure in the politics of Yathrib. His conciliatory skills, when he was a young man, had led to him being called 'the trustworthy one' by the Makkans. These skills, more than his prophetic claims, might have made him attractive to many inhabitants of Yathrib.

Muhammad made plans for his and his followers' flight to Yathrib: eventually, about seventy went. The Prophet almost did not make it. News spread among the Makkans of his agreement at Aqaba. His bitter enemy, Abu Jahl, proposed that he should be stabbed simultaneously by several people, to avoid a vendetta by his followers against one group. Muhammad forestalled this by leaving for Yathrib. Accompanied by Abu Bakr, he arrived there on 24 September 622, after a long, tiring and dangerous journey. The beginning of the Islamic era is reckoned from 16 July, the first day of that year. (Muslims follow a lunar year, slightly shorter than the Western solar calendar.) This event was the *hijra*, or 'emigration', a word that implies separation from old loyalties and attachment to new ones. Yathrib soon became known as Madina, meaning 'the city' of the Prophet.

The Prophet *in* Madina: A Community Leader

Once installed in his new city, Muhammad untethered his camel, which roamed and then came to a halt on waste ground. He dismounted and decided to build his house there, where nobody could claim that another person, Makkan or Madinan, had influenced the Prophet's choice. He bought the site from its owners, and helped put up his lodging himself. It consisted of a rectangular courtyard, with separate cabins for his two new wives. As he married more wives, separate cabins were built for each of them. Muhammad attended to his daily business in the courtyard.

Muhammad's Makkan followers who emigrated to Yathrib were known as the *muhajirun* (emigrants). His local disciples were the *ansar* (helpers). Both groups were Muslims, 'submitters' to the one God, Allah, and obedient to his Prophet, Muhammad. Both the *ansar* and the *muhajirun* worked together to build his house.

A document known as the 'Constitution of Madina' may date, in its essentials, from the early post-*hijra* months. It declares itself to be

> a writing of Muhammad the Prophet between the believers and Muslims of Quraysh and Yathrib and those who follow them and are attached to them and who laboured with them. They are one community to the exclusion of others.

Each group organized its own affairs, under its own chief, based on its own clan tradition. However, relations with outside communities and matters of war and peace were ceded to Muhammad.

Muhammad did not immediately become the leader in Madina, though many Muslim scholars have claimed that he did. For example, the Indian Muslim lawyer and judge, Syed Ameer Ali (1849–1928), who interpreted Islam along modernist lines, maintained that this document 'constituted Mohammed the chief magistrate of the nation'. It

> reveals the Man in his real greatness – a master-mind not only of his own age, . . . but of all ages. No wild dreamer he, bent upon pulling down the existing fabrics of society, but a statesman of unrivalled powers, who in an age of utter and hopeless disintegration, with such materials and such polity as God put ready to his hands, set himself to the task of creating a State, a commonwealth, a society, upon the basis of common humanity. (Ali, *The Spirit of Islam*, 58f.)

Ameer Ali overstated the evidence. Probably this so-called Constitution of Madina enshrines a series of agreements between Muhammad and other groups in the early months and years after his emigration.

Understandably, some Muslims wish to exaggerate Muhammad's influence in Madina upon his arrival there. It enables them to portray opposition to him as wicked: Ameer Ali described Madina as 'honeycombed by sedition and treachery' (ibid., 60). The situation was really quite different. Muhammad had been invited by some Madinans to their city, as an arbitrator who would help reduce factional strife. His reputation as a trustworthy person and as a preacher of God's unity had made a positive impression upon the Madinans who had met him at Aqaba. This led them and many in Madina to hope that he could reconcile factional and warring groups in their city. Even so, not everyone would have welcomed him with open arms. At first the small number of *muhajirun* would not have been large enough or sufficiently confident to impose their will upon dissentient voices. Muhammad had to exercise considerable political and military as well as religious skills over the next few years, before he came to dominate Madina.

Two groups there proved to be thorns in the Prophet's side: some Arabs whom Muslims came to call the *munafiqun* (Q63.1); and Jews. The *munafiqun*, or 'hypocrites', outwardly accepted Islam but had no intention of surrendering any political power or social prestige. Their leader was Abdallah ibn Ubayy, who had hoped to become the leader of Madina before Muhammad's arrival. Most of the town's Jews discounted or even ridiculed the new religious teaching. The Constitution of Madina granted religious freedom to the Jews but demanded their support for Muhammad, should it be needed.

There were pressures upon the Prophet even from among his own followers. As his position gradually strengthened in Madina, quarrels occasionally flared up between the Madinan *ansar* and the Makkan *muhajirun* about who were his best supporters. Moreover, some sources suggest that most of the *ansar* were drawn from the Aws, rather than the Khazraj. These factors required very delicate handling, because of Muhammad's hope that his religious community would transcend the local and narrow loyalties of tribes and clans. He had to reward his devoted followers, but also woo those who were hostile to him and his message.

In Makka, Muhammad could only hope for vindication by God. In Madina, freed from daily harassment by the Quraysh, he could work with God to bring it about. The number of Muslims in Madina may have grown to about one thousand by the end of the first year of the *hijra*. Thus, slowly, a new community came into being in Madina, freed from persecution. It was dependent for its *raison d'être* upon the word of God, not upon tribal customs, however ancient and venerated.

The Quran began to legislate for their communal life. Eventually, Islam was to develop a detailed religious law, based upon the Quran and traditions of the Prophet's words and deeds (see chapter 2, pp. 37–9).

During the Prophet's early days in Madina, three basic duties were imposed.

First, formal daily prayers (*salat*), which had been instituted in Makka, were further regulated. Before the *hijra*, there had been two prayer times: sunrise and sunset (Q20.130, 17.78). Afterwards the Quran mentions intermediate times: 'Glorify God in the evening hour and the morning hour . . . and in the late afternoon, and when the sun goes down' (Q30.17f.). (Most Muslims believe that there are five daily prayer times. Some commentators believe that only three were established during Muhammad's lifetime. The *hadith* have been important in establishing present practice.) Communal prayers were said in the courtyard of Muhammad's dwelling, which is regarded by Muslims as the first mosque (*masjid*, 'place of prostration') in Islam.

The second duty was that of giving alms (*zakat*). This was not voluntary charitable giving, but a kind of tax upon believers that, the Arabic word implies, purifies what is kept for oneself. It was given to the most poor and needy. (Both *salat* and *zakat* are commended and commanded by Q4.162.)

The third duty was the fast of Ramadan, the ninth month of the year. Muslims fast from dawn to dusk throughout that month, but only that month, and refrain during those hours from sexual intercourse. This continued the pre-Islamic practice of a holy time but set it apart from pagan practices. Previously, Ramadan had not been a sacred month. During Ramadan, the clear guidance of the Quran had first been revealed to Muhammad by the angel Jibril, which made it an appropriate month for Muslims to fast in (Q2.185).

These three duties were not the only deeds enjoined upon Muslims by the Quran and the practice of the prophet, though they are very important. From its early days in Madina, such community-building matters as marriage and inheritance (see chapter 4, pp. 79–83) were revealed through Muhammad to Muslims, who had sufficient space and power there to begin to transform themselves into the divine society required by God. The rules of that society cover all aspects of life. The Arabic name for religious law, *Sharia*, means 'the way to a watering hole'. Thus, for a desert people, as Muslims originally were, it is the way to life. It can be argued that, as it developed during the sojourn of the Prophet in Madina and for the first three centuries of Islam, religious law is identical with ethics since, as they walk the way of God's law, Muslims must live uprightly and obediently.

By God's will, Muhammad originated this law. No wonder, then, that he is regarded by Muslims as a model for human ethical behaviour. Western scholars, however, have often interpreted him quite differently, as an immoral, even evil, figure. In particular, he has been unfairly condemned by many of them as a bloodthirsty perpetrator of war. That is a simplistic as well as a defamatory judgement. Quite simply, the situation in Madina and Makka did not permit the Prophet to avoid violence and bloodshed, if he wanted to ensure that the fledgling Muslim community in Madina would survive and flourish.

The Prophet *in* Madina: A Warrior Leader

When he emigrated to Madina, Muhammad must have known that ultimately his vision of God could not endure so long as the Quraysh remained implacably opposed to it and to him, so he took steps to bring matters to a head. The Constitution of Madina condemned the non-believing Quraysh as outlaws, thus making it permissible to wage war on them. Muhammad did not wait long to attack wealthy Makkan caravans as they passed close by Madina. Probably, he had three reasons for this. He had to provide material support for those Makkans who had emigrated with him. Moreover, it no doubt seemed to him just and fitting to get it from those who had rejected him and persecuted his followers. Finally, he was keen to return to his native city as a triumphant prophet, which would prove the truth of his revelation, since all sincere messengers would eventually be vindicated by God.

A raid (*razzia*) was a normal feature of Arab life. *Razzia*s aimed to get plunder from an unfriendly tribe, though one Arab poet confessed that 'if we find no one but our brothers, we fall on them'. Raiders would take camels and other property. They might also kidnap men, women, children, often for ransom. Such raids were often as much a kind of sport as a supplement to economic security. Most nomadic tribes wanted honour and glory even more than victory, and thought treachery to be a matter of shame.

As little blood as possible was shed in raids, so that retaliatory feuds were avoided. If there was bloodshed, the victim's clan could accept compensation. If they were not offered it or refused it, the murderer or a relative could be hunted down and killed, if necessary by a trick. This made stable government difficult to establish, as the conflicting groups in Madina had discovered.

21

Muhammad needed to feed his followers and, ultimately, to defeat the Makkans. He was also intent upon establishing a community bound together in obedience to God, dutiful to his laws and not attached to human whims. He therefore had little sympathy with the chivalrous aspect of the *razzia*. The Quran condemns those who take religion as mere amusement and play (Q7.51), and denies that God created the heavens and the earth as a sport (Q21.16). It teaches that life is to be taken very seriously, as the arena in which to obey or disobey the one God, whose will cannot be thwarted. Muhammad was certain that God's will was that the emerging Muslim community should thrive, and if that were at the expense of pagan, humanist values, so be it. The real problem Muhammad faced was not whether to attack the Makkans but how he could justify it to his followers in the face of strong ancestral taboos. He also had to calculate whether overcoming the economic hardships of the *muhajirun* by raiding Makkan caravans would be worth the inevitable retaliation by a larger force.

Several skirmishes soon took place between Muhammad's followers and caravans from Makka (perhaps they began seven months after the *hijra*). One of them happened during the sacred month of Rajab. A small group of men was sent eastward from Madina. At the end of the second day, they opened sealed orders which ordered them south to Nakhla, on the road between Taif and Makka. They pretended to be pilgrims and joined a Makkan caravan originating in Yemen. A little later, they attacked the guards, during which one Makkan was killed and two more were taken prisoner, though one guard escaped. This raid was afterwards justified by a divine word:

> They [the Prophet's supporters] ask you [Muhammad] about fighting in the holy month. Say: Fighting in it is abhorrent, but more abhorrent in the sight of God is: to bar access to God's way; to deny him; and to prevent access to the holy mosque, driving out its members. Sedition is more abhorrent than slaughter. They will not stop fighting until they turn you from your faith, if they can. Whoever among you turns from faith and dies faithless – their works have failed in this life and the next: these are inhabitants of hellfire, where they will remain forever. (Q2.217)

This verse suggests that the decision to plunder adversaries' caravans during the holy month met with dismay among some of Muhammad's closest followers. The Prophet at first disavowed the raid and refused to accept his share of the booty, until God's revelation clarified the matter. The divine word was that honouring the traditional taboo was less important than punishing the wickedness of the Quraysh for refusing the Prophet's message.

The Makkan pagans were astonished and angered by the Muslims' breach of the sacred month. Moreover, the fact that one of them had been killed in the raid meant that his clan were honour bound to seek revenge or reparation. Perhaps only at this point did those who had been virulently antagonistic to Muhammad's message finally realize how dangerous he was to their long-term interests, and how uninterested he was in playing by the customs and rules which bound their lives.

Early in 624, Muhammad came to know that a rich caravan was returning from Syria to Makka, in the charge of Abu Sufyan, a prominent opponent of the Prophet. The Muslims decided to intercept the caravan. Abu Sufyan learned of this, and diverted the caravan to a safe route. He also sent to Makka for reinforcements. A force of about one thousand people came and fought against some three hundred Muslims at Badr, south-west of Madina. The Muslims fought on firm soil whereas the Makkans had to advance over soft sand dunes. Wind blew sand into the faces of the oncoming Makkans, and the Prophet cried out, 'Gabriel with a thousand angels is falling upon the enemy.' Muhammad's forces showed great bravery and determination, and won the day. Between forty-nine and seventy Makkans were killed, and about fifty prisoners were taken, but only fourteen Muslims died.

Among the Makkan dead was Abu Jahl, the Prophet's bitterest opponent. Muhammad sent his servant for the body, and he cut off the corpse's head and threw it at the feet of his master. Muhammad cried out: 'The head of the enemy of God. Praise God, for there is no other than he!' This was not an expression of the glee of a vengeful and hate-filled man. Rather, it was relief and satisfaction that opposition to God's will had been removed.

Much of sura (chapter) seven of the Quran records God's reflections about the Battle of Badr: this chapter is called 'The Spoils [of War]'. There was a quarrel about the booty. Some claimed the right to keep the weapons of those they had slain. Others, who had guarded Muhammad and thus had no opportunity to plunder, demanded a share of the spoils. The Prophet ordered that all the loot should be collected in one place and distributed equally among the believers. One-fifth of the booty was first allocated to himself, establishing a precedent for future combats, not just in Muhammad's lifetime but since (the fifth portion is taken by whoever is the commander of the faithful).

Events after the battle illustrated the fact that in Muhammad's faithful community (*umma*), old ties were set at nought. His uncle, Abbas, protested against the fact that he was to be ransomed. He claimed that he was a Muslim and had been forced to fight on the side of the idolaters. Muhammad responded; 'God knows best about your being a Muslim, uncle, but to all outward appearances you were fighting against us, so pay your ransom.' Other examples were not so lighthearted. Utba ibn Rabia had been killed in single combat by Hamza, the Prophet's uncle. When his body was dragged to the edge of the great pit into which bodies of the Makkan dead were thrown, Muhammad noticed sadness on the face of his Muslim son, Abu Hudhayfa. He said, 'You feel the death of your father deeply.' The young man said, 'I knew my father to be a wise, virtuous and cultured man. I hoped he would become a Muslim. It saddens me that he died without faith.' This story is yet another illustration that commitment to the monotheistic vision of Islam is more important than other ties, even of blood. It also depicts Muhammad's personal kindness: in the midst of other pressing concerns, he found the time to empathize with Utba's son, and to bless him.

Other sons were less fastidious about putting community before family ties: before the battle began, some urged that their fathers be killed, if found. Their exuberance does not match the consideration and understanding shown by the Prophet towards Utba ibn Rabia's son. It is a fair presumption that Muhammad was deeply anguished by the deaths his policy caused, but that in his mind there was no alternative, given Makkan intransigence to God's will.

By this time, Muhammad no longer believed that it was possible to win over most of the Madinan Jews. After the battle, a Jewish tribe, the Banu Qaynuqa, who lived by trading as goldsmiths, was expelled from Madina, leaving behind their tools and arms.

The Quraysh were bound to retaliate. A year later, Abu Sufyan was put in charge of three thousand men, seven hundred of whom had coats of mail. Each man had a camel for the journey and there were two hundred horses to form a cavalry. The Muslims had only seven hundred men. Abdallah ibn Ubayy kept his three hundred men back in the defence of Madina, arguing that it was folly to go out to fight the enemy. Muhammad may at first have agreed with him, but at length decided, or was prevailed upon, to fight the enemy on open ground at Uhud, a hill to the west of Madina. The Muslims fought bravely, but disaster overtook them when a group of their archers disobeyed orders and abandoned their post to go and look for plunder. Khalid ibn Walid, commander of the Makkan cavalry, wrought havoc among the Muslims. Muhammad was wounded and many of his followers were killed.

Again, a Jewish tribe was singled out for expulsion. Members of the Banu Nadir were accused of plotting to kill Muhammad. They took refuge in their forts, hoping for help from Abdallah ibn Ubayy that did not come. When the Muslims began chopping down their date trees, the Jews surrendered. They were allowed to leave with as much property as they could carry on their camels, except armour. They left bravely, with tambourines, pipes and singing-girls playing behind them. Muhammad appropriated all the plunder and, on this occasion, gave it to the *muhajirun* to the exclusion of the *ansar*. Some of the Jews went to the rich oasis of Khaybar, owned by their co-religionists, about one hundred miles north of Madina, from where they petitioned the Quraysh to avenge them.

As a result, a Makkan army of about ten thousand men set out once more against the Muslims in February and March 627. Muhammad had a trench dug at the vulnerable, southern side of Madina. The Quraysh were not prepared for a long siege. After a fortnight, they squabbled with their confederates, and a heavy storm blew away their tents. Dispirited, they abandoned the so-called Battle of the Ditch (only about twenty people had been killed in stone and arrow attacks) and returned to Makka.

Another Jewish group, the Banu Qurayza, was suspected by the Muslims of being in league with the Quraysh. As a result, the Muslims besieged the suburb of Madina where they lived. After fifteen days, the Qurayza sued for peace, asking to be allowed to depart as the Nadir had. Muhammad would not agree, but allowed them to choose someone to decide their fate. They lighted upon the mortally wounded Sad ibn Muadh, who ordered all the men killed and the women and children sold into slavery. Hearing his decision, Muhammad proclaimed, 'You have judged according to the very sentence of God, who is above the seven skies.' Between six hundred and nine hundred men were beheaded and thrown into a ditch. Again, their property was given only to the *muhajirun*. Later Muslim jurists defended this action because of verses from *sura* 8 of the Quran, which condemn those who break treaties as, it is claimed, the Qurayza had done:

> The worst of beasts in God's sight are unbelievers, who will not believe: those with whom you make a covenant and then they break the covenant every time, lacking the fear of God. So, if you come across them in warfare, deal with them so that those behind them will be scattered; then, they may remember. And, if you fear treachery from such a group, dissolve it [the covenant] with them equally. God does not love the treacherous. (Q8.55–8)

Many non-Muslims are shocked by Muhammad's successes as a warrior leader, and by the political and military successes of the early Islamic community after his death (see chapter 3, pp. 63–6). Although some of Muhammad's responses, for example to the death of Abu Jahl or Sad Ibn Muadh's condemnation of the Banu Qurayza, might seem deplorable to many contemporary non-Muslims, it would be a mistake to picture the Prophet as a bloodthirsty, touchy and hypersensitive leader.

There are a number of mitigating factors. One has to do with the nature of the earliest sources for a life of Muhammad. The Arabs often transmitted stories of the battles and warrior deeds of their kinsmen. Their deeds seemed to cast lustre, even honour, upon them. It is understandable and likely, therefore, that some of the earliest remembrances of the Prophet were about his mighty acts of valour. Maybe even during his lifetime, traditions about his *maghazi* or 'raiding campaigns' began to take shape. Clearly, the life of devotion and commitment to human rights that God and he demanded of his followers was at least as important as his defence against external aggressors. Yet the earliest chroniclers of his life, influenced by traditional ways of remembering great men, may not have seen it that way. Their accounts may have skewed the central features of Muhammad's importance.

Another positive interpretation is to emphasize Muhammad's conformity to the customary practice of his day. So Syed Ameer Ali wrote of Muhammad's treatment of the Banu Qurayza that it was 'an act done in complete accordance with the laws of war as then understood by the nations of the world' (*The Spirit of Islam*, 81). Indeed, it can be argued that Muhammad only allowed such violence as was absolutely necessary for the survival and success of his ministry.

The Quran forbids Muslims to initiate violence, permitting them only to respond to it (Q2.190). Although Muhammad's raids on Makkan caravans were initiated by him, it can credibly be maintained that the Makkans began the spiral of violence when they persecuted Muslims in Makka, and forced them into exile.

When Muhammad took up arms in the way of God, he was not indulging personal pique or a desire for revenge. Stories like that of Utba's son, showing his personal kindness and lack of self-importance, and his deep ethical sensitivity, do not bear out this charge. Certainly, there are many stories of Muhammad's generosity towards his opponents. For example, he spared Abu Azza al-Jumahi after Badr because he was a poor man with a large family. That did not stop Abu Azza, a poet, from accepting bribes from a leader of the Quraysh to spur on other groups to fight the Prophet's army on the occasion of the Battle of Uhud.

Moreover, Muhammad was deeply reluctant to fight, except when he believed it to be absolutely necessary. For example, on the march to Uhud, Abu Dujana, a Muslim and a man of Khazraj, put on his red turban and swaggered up and down between the lines of Muslims. His comrades knew that he meant to kill the enemy. Seeing him, Muhammad said, 'This is a gait which God detests, save at such a time and place as this.'

The Prophet was a reluctant warrior. It is a fair guess that he believed that his opponents, in attacking him and his monotheistic vision, were disobeying the Lord of the worlds whose mouthpiece he was. In the final analysis, those who worked to undermine the Quran's monotheistic message deserved serious retribution. God is not to be mocked, nor, ultimately, can his will be defeated.

It is instructive to record the action of Hind, the daughter of Utba ibn Rabia (and wife of Abu Sufyan), who, after the Battle of Uhud, sought revenge on Hamza. She went to the length of engaging a javelin thrower to kill Hamza. After the battle was over, she scoured the bodies of the dead and wounded for Hamza's corpse. When she found it, she cut out his liver, chewed it and spat it out. This incident puts into perspective the actions of the Prophet that Western, Christian commentators often interpret as mere revenge or bloodlust. Muhammad lived in a society which prized revenge, retaliation and military prowess. What is surprising is the Prophet's willingness to wage war as a means to the end of creating and preserving a monotheistic society, not as an end in itself. Moreover, when eventually he entered Makka in triumph, he forgave Hind and welcomed her into the community of Islam, showing the Prophet's willingness to forgive his and his followers' enemies. Such stories have made Muhammad a revered and much loved figure among Muslims (see also chapter 5, pp. 116–19).

The Prophet Triumphant

Shortly after the Battle of the Ditch, Muhammad announced his intention to make a peaceful pilgrimage to Makka. He gathered fifteen hundred people. The Makkans, alarmed, sent a deputation to meet him at Hudaybiyya, a small oasis just outside Makka. There, a treaty was concluded. Under its terms, Muhammad and his followers agreed to give up their pilgrimage that year, in return for bring allowed to perform a minor pilgrimage (*umra*) the following year. Other terms included a mutual non-aggression pact and a pledge by Muhammad to return to Makka any junior member of the Quraysh who went over to him without the permission of his parent or guardian. The right to become Muslims was granted to any Makkans who wanted to do so. The treaty was to last for ten years. Some of Muhammad's followers grumbled at the concessions he had made, but the astute Prophet knew better. He had dealt with the Quraysh as an equal, and the fact that they were now prepared to negotiate illustrated that they no longer had any stomach for battle.

Muhammad then turned his attention to subduing Jewish resistance. He laid siege to Khaybar. The Jews defended themselves well, but after two months were betrayed and fell into the Prophet's hands. Muhammad showed clemency, demanding that they pay him half the wealth from their agricultural endeavour. They were the first *dhimmi*, those whose lives are bound by 'an agreement of protection' (*dhimma*), under which other monotheists pay a tax (*jizya*) to Muslims in exchange for religious liberty, freedom and protection. The fate of Khaybar led the Jews of Fadak, a nearby oasis, to make a similar agreement with Muhammad, except that the spoils of Khaybar were for all Muslims, whereas the Prophet kept those from Fadak for himself because there had been no need to wage war on it.

Some Muslim historians claim that, around this time, Muhammad sent messages to the Emperors of Byzantium and Abyssinia, and the Kings of Persia and Yemen, demanding that they submit to Islam. Much doubt has been cast on the authenticity of these embassies, but it is quite likely that the Prophet sent messages to the major chiefs of the Arabian peninsula.

In 629, Muhammad and his followers returned to Makka for the first time in seven years. There, they made the minor pilgrimage. A number of prominent Muslims converted, including Khalid bin Walid who later turned his formidable military skills to the Muslim conquests of Persia and Byzantium.

In January 630, a Makkan murdered a Muslim for what appears to have been a personal reason. Muhammad chose to interpret the matter as a breach by the Makkans of the Treaty of Hudaybiyya's stipulation that neither side would attack the other. He assembled an army of ten thousand and marched on Makka. Most Makkans had had enough of warfare. As Muhammad approached the city, Abu Sufyan came to submit to him. Muhammad asked whether he believed that there was no god but God. It is said that he received the brave, equivocal and rueful answer, 'If there had been any other god, he might have helped me.' Muhammad continued, 'Isn't it time for you to recognize that I am the Messenger of God?' Abu Sufyan responded, 'As far as that goes, I still have my doubts.' He knew when to bow to the inevitable, though. He returned to the city with terms of surrender. His wife, Hind, screamed curses at him: 'Don't take any heed of this fat old fool. A fine defender of his people he has turned out to be.' But her husband persuaded most of the townspeople to shelter in their homes or the Kaba, where Muhammad had promised most could take refuge when he entered Makka.

Muhammad entered Makka in triumph, with scarcely any resistance against him. He went to the Kaba and kissed the black stone. He ordered all idols in the shrine to be shattered. However, he gave instructions that representations of Jesus and Mary were to be spared, and for the walls of the building to be washed with water from Zamzam, a sacred well within its precincts. Bilal sounded the *adhan*, 'the call to pray', and the Muslims formed serried ranks within the Kaba and prayed there. Muhammad proved a merciful conqueror, sparing all save a few. One person who was executed was Suhayl ibn Amr, who had negotiated the Treaty of Hudaybiyya for the Makkans and had refused to insert into the preamble the phrase 'Muhammad, Prophet of God'. Muhammad was always jealous of the truth and uniqueness of his prophetic status. He had reason to be. Other claimants lay in wait to take advantage of his success. One was called Maslama (which Muslims contemptuously rendered in its diminutive form, Musaylima) from the mainly Christian tribe of Hanifa in the centre of Arabia. He is said to have written a letter to Muhammad, addressing both of them as 'Messengers of God'. The Prophet replied, acknowledging himself as such a messenger, but calling Maslama 'the liar'. There was not room in Arabia for two prophets of God's unity. Muhammad also condemned to death two singing-girls who had satirized him. He sometimes found it difficult to accept the barbs of irony and ridicule. He was a serious prophet of a God who creates nothing in idleness or sport.

Muhammad was now the ruler of the Hijaz. He did not stay long in Makka, but returned to Madina after two weeks. In the last two years of his life, he consolidated Islam's sway in the Arabian peninsula: Taif, Oman, Bahrain, Yemen, Hadhramaut, Kinda, in northern Arabia, and many other places submitted to the rule of the Prophet and the religion of the one God that he brought.

Some Arabian tribes that had recently submitted to Muhammad and Islam considered that his death in June 632 relieved them of the responsibility of faith and obedience. That September, Khalid ibn Walid, the so-called 'sword of Islam', crushed their revolt. Plans were also afoot among the Muslims to extend the religion of God and his Prophet. Shortly before his death, Muhammad had commanded a force to invade towns in Transjordan, on the borders of Byzantium. Two weeks after his death, his wishes were carried out. The following year, Muslim armies went forth in faith and hope: Khalid attacked the Persian Empire; and Yazid, the son of a man who had once been Muhammad's bitter enemy, Abu Sufyan, went forth against the Eastern Roman Empire. Armies disintegrated before their advance. The Persian Empire finally succumbed in 641.

In 637, the caliph, Umar, entered Jerusalem in triumph. The holiest city of Judaism and Christianity was now under the control of the servants of the latest revelation of Semitic monotheism. For Muslims, however, Jerusalem is merely the third most sacred city, after Makka, where the Prophet was born, and Madina, where he had become a political leader and where, at length, he died and was buried.

Muhammad *and the* Unity *of* God

Muslims believe that the unity of God should be mirrored by the unity of the *umma* (community). This chapter examines the Quran's teaching about the prophethood of Muhammad. It investigates how the Quran and Muhammad, its human receptacle of communication, undergird the community of Islam. It describes divergent interpretations of what it means to be *muslim*, 'one who submits [to God]'. This raises the question whether such diversity is legitimate, or else an illicit and impious response to the clear commands of God.

The Seal *of the* Prophets

The Quran teaches that God has sent a series of messengers and prophets, from Adam to Muhammad. They were not sent to save human beings as isolated individuals, though each person has to make choices that decide his or her ultimate destiny in heaven or hell. Mortal men, women and children can only be securely preserved from this world's trials and woes within a community that faithfully obeys the will of the one God.

The word 'messenger' (in Arabic, *rasul*) is used of men who went to many different communities to preach the unity of God, and the certainty of the Day of Judgement when polytheists would undoubtedly go to hell. Although every messenger is necessarily a prophet (in Arabic, *nabi*), the opposite is not true. Twenty-eight prophets are recorded in the Quran: all of them, except Muhammad, are men written about in the Jewish and Christian scriptures.

Muhammad's supremely important prophetic role is attested by Muslims and witnessed to by the Quran: he is the 'seal of the prophets' (Q33.40). This may originally have meant simply that he stood within a monotheistic Semitic tradition of faith which believed that God revealed his word to and through particular human beings. Most Muslims interpret this to mean that, after Muhammad, there could be renewers and reformers but no more prophets. Mystics and some others have also understood it to refer to Muhammad's exceedingly close relationship to God, so that of all humankind, he was nearest to God and his will (see chapter 2, pp. 43–9).

Jews and Christians have no monopoly on monotheism. Indeed, in the view of the Quran, Muhammad, and developed Islamic thought, they have been poor practitioners of it (see, for example, chapter 3, pp. 54–9). Maybe, then, the word *nabi* originally denoted the fact that Muhammad continued and reformed the Judaeo–Christian tradition. The word *rasul*, which embraces other messengers, too, such as the Arabs Hud and Salih, suggests something even more interesting: namely, that Muhammad summed up a history of more universal monotheism that pre-dates Judaism and Christianity, and includes the Arabs.

That tradition originated with Abraham (in Arabic, 'Ibrahim') who, according to the Quran, 'was neither a Jew nor a Christian. He was a monotheist [*hanif*], one who surrenders to God [a *muslim*], and not a polytheist' (Q3.67). Abraham was undoubtedly the most important prophet before Muhammad. There are parallels between them: in particular, both were intent upon establishing a rigorous monotheism. To this end, both stood out against the polytheism of their close relations: Muhammad condemned the pagan beliefs of his grandfather, whereas Abraham spurned those of his father (Q19.41–50). Abraham was willing to sacrifice his son at the one God's command. (According to Muslim tradition, the son whom Abraham was willing to kill was Ishmael, not Isaac as the Hebrew Bible records. The Quran does not mention the lad's name.) This must have struck a poignant chord in

Muhammad's heart, who knew how men yearned after sons. He himself had no male offspring who survived infancy. He was taunted by his Makkan opponents for this lack. When his son was born to Mariya the Copt about April 630, he named him Ibrahim, after his great predecessor, but the little boy died before his first birthday.

Abraham had been the originator under God of the tradition of Arabian monotheism, but Muhammad brought it to its true realization. The Quran records that Abraham visited Makka with his son, Ishmael, and prayed that it would be made a secure and fruitful land. There, they raised the foundations of the Kaba. When Muhammad entered the Kaba in triumph in 630, he must have reflected that, whereas Abraham had built the Kaba and purified it, he was purging it of pagan associations and restoring a pristine monotheism (Q2.125–7).

The Status *and* Integrity *of the* Quran

The Quran is the guarantee that the message given to and through Muhammad is God's final and successful word of truth to humankind. Muslims believe that the Quran is a luminously true scripture, because God has said so in it. It is often described as 'the Clear Sign' (e.g. Q98.1f.), and is held to be the last scripture given to the final prophet. All Muslims believe that the Quran is divine in origin. The revelations delivered piecemeal by Gabriel to Muhammad for over twenty years form part of 'the Mother of the Book' (Q13.39). This primordial revelation is also called 'the well-preserved Tablet' (Q85.22), a designation which suggests that it is guarded from corruption.

On the 'Night of Power' (*laylat al-qadr*), the twenty-seventh day of the month of Ramadan, the revelation descended to the lowest of the seven heavens. From there it was given to Muhammad from time to time, as and when circumstances demanded (Q97.1–5; 17.105f.). The Night of Power has a special place in Muslim devotion. It is regarded as better than one thousand months (Q97.3). Many a Muslim man will spend that night in a mosque. There, a person who knows how to recite the Quran in Arabic and by heart (in Arabic, a *hafiz*) will do so before dawn.

For Muslims, the Quran is the word of God, faithfully received and transmitted by Muhammad. However, there are stories from the earliest years of Islam that pose questions about the Prophet's personal involvement in the creation of the Quran. They usually arise out of situations where the revelation seems to have been convenient to his religious policy or personal lifestyle. The Quran itself witnesses to the fact that Muhammad was enticed to overstep the mark in adapting his message to his Makkan audience:

> If we [God] had not strengthened you, you would almost have bent somewhat towards them. In which case, we would have made you to taste an identical measure [of punishment?] in this life, and an identical measure after death. Furthermore, you would have found nobody to help you against us. (Q17.76f.)

Tabari recounts the story of a supposed revelation from God, which Muhammad soon came to realize was no such thing. This is the famous event of the Satanic Verses. Tabari tells it twice, with two different emphases. One report (perhaps the most commonly accepted of the two) stresses the fact that Muhammad longed to attract the Makkans to his message. Satan realized that he was eager to effect a reconciliation with his people. When God revealed the words 'Have you considered al-Lat, al-Uzza and Manat, the third, the other' (Q53.19f.), Satan put on Muhammad's tongue 'these are exalted *gharaniq*, whose intercession is permitted'. ('Numidian cranes' is probably the translation of *gharaniq*. They were auspicious birds, said to fly at a great height.) The Quraysh were very pleased. Those of them who were in the mosque at the time these words were uttered prostrated themselves in prayer when they heard their deities mentioned. However, Gabriel chastised the Prophet for reading words to the people that he had not brought him. Muhammad was distressed but God sent him a reassuring revelation: any subconscious temptation Muhammad felt to elaborate or even invent revelation merely illustrated his prophetic credentials, for messengers before him had been similarly tempted:

> We never sent a prophet or a messenger before you but, when he desired something, Satan tampered with that desire. But God will cancel anything Satan interjects, and will confirm his signs. For God is full of knowledge and wisdom. (Q22.52)

God then annulled the verses from the Quran, and scorned the very existence of these goddesses, saying that Muhammad's contemporaries and their ancestors had merely made up their existence (Q53.23).

The Quraysh became even more violently hostile to Muhammad and his followers.

There are problems about the historicity of this story. Many Western scholars believe that Ibn Hisham, the editor of Ibn Ishaq's work, removed it, because he found it embarrassing. Others, however, believe it to be a fable devised to explain Q22.52. Many Muslims tend to disbelieve it, since it is not found in the early biography of the Prophet by Ibn Ishaq. Neither is it in the traditions (*hadith*) about the Prophet's words and deeds gathered by Bukhari and Muslim in the ninth century. It is, however, difficult to understand why such a perplexing story should have been invented by a pious Muslim like Tabari, even to explain a difficult verse, or why it should have been included in his work, if he had any reason to doubt its authenticity.

Tabari's other version of the occasion of this controversial revelation underlines the fact that Muhammad was seeking political leadership in Makka. A tradition, that of a man named Abu al-Aliyah, puts this interpretation most succinctly: the Quraysh would admit Muhammad into the charmed circle of the really powerful if he made mollifying comments about the three deities. This variant has been dismissed by some modern Western biographers. They believe that this event happened too early (*c.*615) in Muhammad's career for him to have formulated the idea of a divine society, modelled on the commands of the one God. It is hard to see much merit in their argument, since this seems to have been the import of God's word to Muhammad from the very beginning.

Western non-Muslims have often used this incident to depict Muhammad in an unfavourable light. However, it need not do so. In Tabari's accounts of this incident, the Satanic Verses were diabolical insinuations into the Prophet's mind, an attempt by Satan to undermine Muhammad's ability to distinguish between his desires and God's word. Yet this temptation came to naught. The Prophet had sufficient insight and integrity to realize that he was being hoodwinked, and sufficient faith that God would rescue him from his error. So the account of the Satanic Verses, rather than witnessing to Muhammad's gullibility or even his deceitfulness, could be used to illustrate his complete integrity, and thus his singular appropriateness as the apt vehicle for the pure word of God.

News of the rapprochement between Muhammad and his Makkan opponents had reached Muslim emigrants in Abyssinia, where they had been only two months. Immediately, they set off back to Makka. On their approach to the city, they were greeted with the news that the Prophet's recantation had made matters even worse for the Muslims. So, although they entered Makka, they did so either secretly or after receiving the protection of a relative or friend. They had gone to Abyssinia primarily to escape persecution. The Prophet may also have hoped that, safe there from persecution, this small group could aim to govern its life by the will of God. When the exiles thought that Muhammad had acquired a measure of real power in Makka, they returned to set up an obedient Islamic community (umma) under his direct authority. They were thwarted by his change of mind, and had to wait a few more years before such a society could be established in a safe place, Madina.

The account of the Satanic Verses illustrates the fact that, from early in his ministry, Muhammad aimed to establish a community, protected from Makkan persecution, which would be obedient to his monotheistic vision. Yet it soon became clear to him that his attempt to compromise with Makkan idol worshippers undermined his central belief in the oneness of God. He therefore abandoned negotiations and concessions, even though his aim to create a monotheistic community suffered a temporary setback.

As for claims that Muhammad manufactured revelation because it suited him to do so, no Muslim would agree to this, and many non-Muslims now accept his sincerity, even if their interpretation of his experiences differs from his. Muhammad seems genuinely to have believed that he was the obedient transmitter of revelation that came from outside himself, ultimately from the Lord of the worlds. It is difficult to suppose that a man who saw himself as the prophetic servant of that one God should have tampered with, still less invented, divine words of guidance. Occasionally, some of his contemporaries alluded to the convenience of some of his revelations. For example, some years later in Madina his young wife Aisha famously made a sarcastic remark about God hastening to do Muhammad's pleasure (chapter 4, p. 89). But as often as not, the prophecy vouchsafed to Muhammad was not convenient. It did not provide Muhammad with economic security, social acceptance or worldly power, when he first left the security of Khadija's caravans for the dread uncertainties of a prophetic vocation.

The Sources *of* Sunni Islam

Upon Muhammad's death, the ideal of a monotheistic community guided by the will of God had been established. In embryo, much (most Muslims would say, all) legislation undergirding that divine society was in place: the Quran had, for example, legislated for marriage and inheritance, the rhythm of corporate and personal prayer and piety, war and peace, and relations with other communities (see chapter 1, pp. 20–1). But the details of these and other pressing needs were not laid down.

The Quran addressed the fledgling Muslim community based, until the very end of the Prophet's life, in Makka and Madina. When, shortly thereafter, Muslims conquered North Africa, West Asia and part of Western Europe, Muslims faced new cultures and situations that the Quran had not dealt with. When Muslims asked themselves how they could be faithful to the monotheistic vision in these new circumstances, the Quran itself offered clues. It states: 'God and his angels send blessings on the Prophet. Believers, bless him and salute him with deepest respect' (Q33.56). It further adjures: 'You certainly have an excellent pattern in the Prophet of God' (Q33.21), who 'never speaks whimsically' (Q53.3).

Consequently, Muhammad's deeds and words have become a source of inspiration second only to the Quran itself. Prophecy ended with his death, but his life provides Muslims with indications of how they can faithfully construct their living and dying within an Islamic *umma*. It has become the practice of Muslims to model their lives on his.

A story about Muhammad is called a *hadith*, which means 'news', though the usual English translation is 'tradition'. A *hadith* is an oral tradition that describes a deed or saying of the Prophet. Some traditions also record sayings and deeds of the earliest followers of Muhammad: because they modelled their lives so closely on his, Muslims believe that their example and witness can be emulated by believers.

Each *hadith* about Muhammad has two parts. The first is the *isnad*, a chain of authorities at its beginning, which lists people through whom the story is passed across the generations. The original authority is always a close follower, friend and contemporary of Muhammad. The substance of each story, the main text, is called the *matn*, which provides a word of guidance for Muslims then and now. Here is an example of a *hadith*, without the, often long, list of authorities:

> It is narrated on the authority of Abdallah son of Umar (may God be pleased with them) that the Holy Prophet (may the peace of God be upon him) said: Islam is raised on five [pillars], i.e. the oneness of God, the establishment of prayer, payment of *zakat*, the fast of Ramadan, pilgrimage [to Makka]. A person said [to the narrator]: which of the two precedes the other – pilgrimage or the fast of Ramadan? Upon this he [the narrator] replied: No, the fasts of Ramadan precede the pilgrimage.

The five pillars of Islam, though mentioned in brief in the Quran, are clarified and developed by the *hadith*. Thus, even after death, the Prophet guided and directed the ongoing life of the community, through the oral transmission of his words and deeds, which were eventually edited and written down.

This tradition is preserved by Muslim (*c*.817–75). He and, especially, al-Bukhari (810–70) are the most famous compilers of *hadith*. Their collections and four others are generally regarded as authentic by Muslims.

Hadith provided material for lives of Muhammad. The most famous early life was that of Ibn Ishaq (*c*.704–*c*.767), whose material was edited into its most popular form by Ibn Hisham (d. *c*.828). The *hadith* and the Quran form the basis of Muslim law, the *Sharia*, the divine highway on which those who travel can know that they obey God.[1]

Thus, the life of the Prophet and the sanctity of his words and deeds have been deeply woven into the structure of Sunni Islam, which is followed by the vast majority of Muslims.

Muslims carefully distinguish Muhammad's words from Quranic revelation. They make a further distinction within the *hadith* between *hadith qudsi* and *hadith nabawi*. The former, 'a holy tradition' records God's own utterances, which the Prophet referred to but which do not form part of the Quran. The latter, 'prophetic tradition', are Muhammad's personal sayings. These may be venerated, but they are the Prophet's opinion, not God's command.

1. Details of the formation of Muslim law can be found in Watt, *A Short History of Islam*, chapter 4.

A tradition originating with one of Muhammad's wives, Umm Salama, emphasizes that Muhammad could make mistakes when he made decisions without a direct word from God. The Prophet said:

> I am only human being, and you bring your disputes to me some perhaps being more eloquent in their pleas than others, so that I give judgement on their behalf according to what I hear from them. Therefore whatever I decide for anyone which by right belongs to his brother he must not take, for I am granting him only a portion of hell. (Robson (trans.), *Mishkat al-masabih*, vol. 1, 800f.)

Yet the opinions of the 'seal of the prophets' (Q33.40) are not to be treated lightly, and they guide the believer when there is no clear quranic injunction.

When Muhammad died, revelation ceased. He could not be succeeded as a prophet, but his community needed a temporal leader to guide and sustain it. Abu Bakr (632–4) was appointed *khalifa* (successor to Muhammad as political leader of the Muslims). After him came Umar (634–44), Uthman (644–56) and Ali (656–61). These are known as the four 'rightly-guided caliphs' (*rashidun*) and this early period is looked upon by Sunni Muslims as a golden age.

Even so, most Muslim and Western scholars of Islam locate the beginnings of Muslim sectarian controversies in the period of the *rashidun* caliphs. Sunni Muslims believe that Sunni Islam began when Abu Bakr was appointed. He initiated the process of collecting the Quran, the first stage in the creation of Muslim law, which was finally in place by the early tenth century.

Conservative Sunni Muslims do not believe that the establishment of the *Sharia* was a process of innovative development over two centuries. In their view the *Sharia* was the logical drawing out of what was already essentially in place upon the death of the Prophet. True, a limited diversity is permitted within the broad framework of Sunni Islam: four slightly different law schools exist, and every Sunni Muslim belongs to one of them. Yet there is an overarching unity that binds together Sunni Muslims, from Morocco to Indonesia: laws about, for example, what one may eat and wear, how to worship, and whom one can marry, are broadly similar wherever one travels in the *dar al-Islam* ('the household [or 'abode'] of Islam', areas in which the majority of people are subject to the divine law).

An Alternative Way: Shia Islam

Several facts, however, thwart the Sunni Muslim contention that it provides the logical unfolding of Islam as God and the Prophet intended it to be. The most important is the existence of sundry alternative persuasions and routes. These are held by those who believe passionately that their way is a more exact submission to the revelation of Islam. Among the most important of these divers translations of Muhammad's vision of a monotheistic community united in obedience to God are the adherents of the Shia way.

Shia Muslims, who number about eleven per cent of the world's Muslims, also trace their origins to the earliest period of Islamic history. The word 'Shia' means 'party' or 'faction [of Ali]'. They believe that the Prophet's son-in-law Ali, husband of Fatima, should have succeeded Muhammad as the political and spiritual head of the Muslim community. They point to the occasion a few weeks before Muhammad's death when, returning with many Muslim followers from his final pilgrimage to Makka, he stopped at the oasis of Ghadir Khomm. He took Ali's hand and said, 'Whoever I protect, Ali also is his protector. O God, be a friend to whoever is his friend and an enemy to whoever is his enemy.' Shia Muslims interpret this as Muhammad's designation of Ali as his rightful successor. Sunni Muslims, if they consider this event at all, regard it as the Prophet's support for Ali in some internal conflict. They claim that, on his deathbed, Muhammad appointed Abu Bakr and not Ali to lead the prayers, thus showing his favour towards his close ally and friend.

In the Shia view, the descendants of Muhammad through his daughter Fatima and her husband Ali possess spiritual power in excess of the merely temporal authority that Sunni Muslims grant the caliph. The Sunni conviction, however, is that the best man from the Quraysh ought to have led the community, which should be guided by obedience to the *Sharia*, not to the spiritual and political illumination of Muhammad's closest relatives. Ali's death at the hands of an assassin in 661 was followed by that of his son and Muhammad's grandson, Husayn, at the Battle of Karbala in 680, at the hand of forces loyal to Muawiya's son, Yazid. Ever since, Shia Muslims have dwelt on concepts of martyrdom, self-sacrifice, and nostalgic ruminations about what might have been if Ali, the noblest of men, had rightfully succeeded his father-in-law as head of all Muslims.

Indeed, Ali is often painted by Shia sources in glowing terms that quite put Muhammad's virtues into the shade. Later Shia mythology made ever more elaborate claims for the spiritual omnicompetence of the descendants of Muhammad through Ali and Fatima. Even so dedicated a modernist as Ameer Ali, himself a Shia Muslim, wrote glowingly of Ali:

> On Osman's [more properly, Uthman's] tragical death [in 656], Ali was elected to the vacant Caliphate by the consensus of the people. The rebellions which followed are a matter of history . . . The dagger of an assassin destroyed the hope of Islam . . . Seven centuries before, this wonderful man would have been apotheosised; thirteen centuries later his genius and talents, his virtues and his valour, would have extorted the admiration of the civilised world. As a ruler, he came before his time. He was almost unfitted by his uncompromising love of truth, his gentleness, and his merciful nature, to cope with the Ommeyades' [more properly, Umayyads'] treachery and falsehood. (Ali, *The Spirit of Islam*, 283)

Yet history seriously interrogates the Shia myth of origins, not least in raising the issue of Ali's competence to rule. He was passed over twice as caliph and when he was finally chosen, many Muslims would not accept him, despite Ameer Ali's tendentious claim to the contrary. The reasons for this are various. One was that he stood between other Muslims and their aspirations for political power. Another was, arguably, his lack of political judgement, which he urgently needed if he was to keep the community together and himself in control of it. His weak position and his indecisiveness caused the first major split in Islam. The Kharijites (from *khawarij*, 'those who seceded') condemned him for agreeing to arbitration after the Battle of Siffin in 657, instead of seeking the judgement of God upon his enemies. They were later joined by other former supporters of Ali from Kufa, a city in Iraq, where Ali was assassinated by one of them.

Thus a case can be made that Ali was appointed above his capability, and that this was known by many of his contemporaries who resisted his caliphal pretensions as long as possible. Certainly, many Sunni Muslims, in their own myth of origins, regard him as the least, as well as the last, of the rightly-guided caliphs.

Nevertheless, the Shia judgement that the family of the Prophet possesses unique charismatic and authoritative power over the believers establishes, in a very different way from Sunni Islam, the central importance of Muhammad in the construction of Muslim obedience to

God. In this view, his charismatic and exemplary life, his acute spiritual discernment, but also his family ties, validate the faith of Muslims.

Shia Muslims differ from Sunni interpreters of Islam not only on the issue of who should have succeeded the Prophet and with what authority, but also on matters of law, authority and quranic exegesis. Mainstream Shia Muslims believe that twelve descendants (called Imams) of Muhammad rightfully followed him as leaders of the Islamic community. The last one, Muhammad al-Qaim, went into periods of *ghayba* 'occultation' from 874, and his final return is still expected by them. Meanwhile, they follow a *marja al-taqlid* (source of imitation), whom they personally choose. He must be a *mujtahid* (a theologian recognized by his teachers as fit to carry out the effort of interpreting religious law). By virtue of their relationship with the *marja al-taqlid*, all 'twelver' Shia Muslims feel personally and mystically linked to the twelfth Imam and the Prophet.

A distinctive quranic exegesis of many Shia Muslims is called *tawil* or allegory. They trace this back to their early leaders, whom they believe had specialized, secret knowledge. They justify this knowledge from the verses 'God has taught the bee . . . A multi-hued drink comes out of their bodies' (Q16.68f.). They understand this liquid to be the Quran, and call Ali 'commander of the bees'. Some Shia Muslims, especially the Ismailis, believe that the Quran has both an exoteric (*zahir*) interpretation, but also an esoteric, inner meaning (*batin*), known only to them. Thus they are privy to a secret dimension of Islam, known only to a few. Obviously, this leads them into a questionable sense of superiority over ordinary Muslims. (Ismailis follow the branch of Shia Islam called after Ismail, the seventh and, in their view, last descendant of the Prophet to succeed him as leader of the community. They are now split into many factions.) Ismaili convictions make great play with cyclical and cosmological theories of history based on the number seven. The constraints upon their quranic exegesis seem few and ineffable: in their interpretation of the divine word, it is far from the 'clear sign' it claims to be.

Mystic Paths

The esoteric interpretation of the Quran practised by many Shia Muslims is not the only form of mysticism in Islam. The most popular expression of Islamic mysticism has been Sufi Islam.

The derivation of the word 'Sufi' is uncertain. It is claimed that it comes from the Greek word *sophos*, which means 'wise', or the Arabic word *suf*, meaning 'wool'. It may be that the word 'Sufi' was, from its beginnings, a pun, combining both the senses of wise and wool. Clearly, Christian influence was involved in the beginnings of popular Islamic mysticism, as were other non-Islamic elements. The word *sophos* was drawn from Eastern Christian spirituality, and the word *suf* may refer not only to the woollen garments worn by early Muslim mystics but also to the likelihood that they borrowed this practice from their Christian spiritual counterparts.

However, Sufism is grounded in the Quran and the life of the Prophet by its Muslim practitioners. Nowadays, various individuals and groups call themselves Sufis, influenced by New Age ideas or the 'pick and mix' attitude towards religion encouraged by trivial forms of postmodernism. This is a bogus claim. Sufism is not rootless, individualistic and abstruse beliefs and practices. It is soaked in the language of the Quran and devotion to the Prophet.

If Sunni Muslims believe that Muhammad was the supreme lawgiver, and Shia Muslims see him as the first in a line of charismatic, related individuals who guide the community, Sufis regard him as a mystic. A very early revelation describes him as 'enmantled' (Q74.1), a state of dress associated with mystics. Some Muslims have argued that the so-called 'abbreviated letters' found in various combinations at the beginning of twenty-nine *suras* have a mystic import. These isolated letters may suggest the speech-effort made by the Prophet as he began articulating God's word: noises like (for example) the letters *a*, *l* and *r* (found at the beginning of *suras* 10, 11, 12, 14 and 15) issued from his lips as he began to recite. This is an attractive though unprovable supposition. However, Muhammad's conviction that he spoke God's word surely betokens mystical experience: it is not a common occurrence, to be explained solely in rational terms! Sometimes *hadith* record that there were outward manifestations accompanying the Prophet's interior reception of revelation: he would feel pain, in his ears would be a noise like a clanging bell, onlookers would see great beads of sweat drip down his forehead.

The Quran (Q17.1) describes a night journey from Makka to a mosque in Jerusalem, which Muslims believe to have been undertaken by the Prophet in a state of rapture. This event is much elaborated in the *hadith*. He was visiting his cousin, Umm Hani, who lived near the Kaba. One night he went there to recite the Quran. Afterwards, he went to sleep in the *hijr*, an enclosed area to the north-west of the Kaba. He was woken up by Gabriel, at whose insistent prompting he mounted a white beast, something between a mule and an ass, named Buraq. With Gabriel beside him, the Prophet sped beyond Madina (then still Yathrib; this incident is usually dated to *c.*620) and Khaybar, until they reached Jerusalem. There they were met by several prophets, Abraham, Moses and Jesus among them. Muhammad was joined by them as he prayed on the site of the Temple. He acted as prayer-leader, with the others behind him. He accepted a container of milk and drank from it, but refused a pitcher of wine. Then, like Enoch, Elijah, Jesus and Mary before him, Muhammad mounted Buraq from the temple rock and was taken up into the seven heavens, accompanied by Gabriel. As they passed each stage, they saw a great prophet: Adam; Jesus and John the Baptist; Joseph; Enoch; Aaron and Moses; and finally Abraham. Reflecting later upon this experience, Muhammad is said to have uttered: 'I was a prophet when Adam was still between water and clay.'

The summit of his ascent was the lote tree, beyond which is a hidden mystery, unknown to any save God. Gabriel appeared to him in his undimmed archangelic splendour. Then the divine light descended upon the lote tree, covering it, and the eye of Muhammad gazed upon it without flinching. There, he received the command that his people should pray fifty prayers a day. On his descent with Gabriel, Moses told him to return and get the number decreased. Moses kept sending him back until the number was five. Moses still urged him to return, but the Prophet said: 'I have returned to my Lord and asked until I am ashamed. I will not go again.' Muslims interpret this tradition to mean that God does not impose impossible burdens on his people, but only manageable ones.

When he returned and recounted this event to his Makkan opponents, they mocked him. However, Muslims then and now find it a source of joy and wonder, a confirmation of Muhammad's status as the seal of the prophets. Abu Bakr was one of his stoutest defenders against pagan calumnies that he was deranged. Muhammad thereafter called him as-Siddiq, 'the great witness of truth'. This story has decisively affected the course of Islamic devotional beliefs and practices. Some Muslims believe that Muhammad made the night journey and ascension (in Arabic, *miraj*) through the seven heavens in the body. However, most discern in it a deeply spiritual and mystical experience. It is celebrated every year on 27 Rajab. Sufis have creatively engaged with its importance and meaning. Many believe that it is described in the Quran:

> Indeed he saw him at a second descent, near the lote tree of the boundary; close by is the garden of refuge. The lote tree was shrouded. His eye did not avert, nor did it rove. Truly, he saw the greatest of his Lord's signs. (Q53.13–18)

The *miraj* lends itself to various interpretations. Many see the ascension as a profound experience of God's love towards his friend, Muhammad. The fact that Gabriel could not accompany the Prophet beyond the lote tree lest he burn his wings (so mystics avow), is a reminder that the archangel remains a veil between the lover and his beloved that must be torn away. So Muhammad is left alone in a loving encounter with God, and says, 'I have a time with God in which no created being has access, not even Gabriel who is pure spirit.' Even so, Muhammad remains a human being (the quranic verse about the night journey calls him a servant). This encourages Sufis to believe that they too can enter the presence of the divine beloved.

Muhammad remains the perfect man for mystics, many of whom believe that his life was surrounded by miracles, although he himself claimed that his only miracle was the transmission of the Quran. A mystic called Muqatil ibn Sulayman (d. 767) interpreted the second sentence of the quranic 'Light Verse' (Q24.35) as referring to Muhammad: his light shines through other prophets. The idea of the light of Muhammad became widespread by the beginning of the tenth century, with many interpretations of what it meant. Furthermore, from the twelfth century onwards, it became customary to celebrate the birthday of Muhammad, on 12 Rabi al-Awwal. On this occasion, Muslims still write songs, prayers, and poems in honour of and with love for their Prophet. A virtue was made of Muhammad's illiteracy (Muslims claim that this is what the reference to him as *ummi* means in Q7.157, though this is a controversial translation; it may mean 'non-Jewish' or 'gentile'): he was the model of unsullied love and submission, not of detached reasoning.

Many Sufis reverently allude to the *hadith qudsi*, '*ana Ahmad bila mim*', 'I am Ahmad [which means Muhammad; he is so-called in Q61.6] without the letter *m*'. That letter, and only that letter, which many Sufis interpret as the letter of creatureliness, limitation and death, separates the Prophet (whose coming as Ahmad is predicted by Jesus in Q61.6) from *ahad*, which means 'one', namely God, the monotheistic Lord of creation. This divine saying has been used by many poets in the eastern Islamic world. There, ordinary Muslims, who are deeply influenced by Islam's mystical movements, often repeat traditional wordplays on *ahad* and 'Ahmad', symbolizing the importance to them of God and Muhammad. Thus Muhammad becomes closely linked with God, almost in a symbiotic relationship, though orthodox Muslims follow the Quran in denying that God has a son (e.g. Q2.116).

Given the esoteric interpretations of many Sufis, it is no wonder that many Sunni Muslims hold them in great suspicion, especially when they seem to compromise or even deny the unity of God and his distinction from all his creatures, even so great a one as Muhammad. Sunni Muslims emphasize the unknowability of God, whom they obey by following the highway of divine command outlined in the Quran. They do not encourage beliefs that the Prophet is exemplary in his friendly, even intimate, relationship with God.

One person who did much to make Sufism respectable to Sunni Muslims was Abu Hamid Muhammad al-Ghazali (1058–1111). He taught Islamic theology and philosophy in Baghdad. One day in 1095, he was struck silent while teaching. Moderns might call his a psychosomatic illness, but this explains nothing very important. Six months earlier he had written *Tahafut al-falasafa* (The Refutation of the Philosophers). In it he denounced the claims (unjustified in his view) of metaphysical theology and philosophy to knowledge that was properly the preserve of God. His was, literally, a crisis of integrity, which struck him dumb. He wrote, 'My feet were standing on a sandbank which was slipping beneath me, and I saw that I was in danger of hellfire if I did not do something to change my ways.' He went on pilgrimage to Makka, and retired to his birthplace, Tus in Khurasan, where he lived as a Sufi. He returned to writing and (briefly) teaching. He spent his last years integrating the mystic, ascetic and academic. Although his importance as an Islamic intellectual and Sufi practitioner has been called into question, at the very least he is an example of an eminent figure who combined, in his later years, a Sufi lifestyle with a commitment to orthodox Islamic teaching. He refutes those who contend that Sufism is inevitably predisposed to *bida*, 'innovation', which is the unacceptable opposite of *sunna*, the 'trodden path' or 'customary practice' of those who follow the teachings of the Prophet.

Many Sufi orders arose in the period after al-Ghazali's death. The inspirer of one such order was Jalal al-Din Rumi (1207–73), a Persian Sufi poet. This fellowship, originating in Turkey, was the *mawlawiyya*, the 'whirling dervishes'. Their dance, on one interpretation, attempts to symbolize the motions of the spheres. Rumi himself explained that:

> Why do I have to dance in the glow of his [God's] sun?
> So that when the speck of dust dances he may remember me.
> (Quoted in Baldick, *Mystical Islam*, 91)

Rumi wrote a lengthy and celebrated poem, the *Mathnawi*, which glorifies the divine beloved. He had found its image in a wandering dervish called Shams al-Din, whom he first met in 1244. For a while, the two men lived in the same house and were inseparable. Rumi's son, Sultan Walad, likened his father's relationship with this 'hidden saint' to the mysterious journey of Moses with Khadir (or Khidr), described in the Quran (Q18.65–82). Khadir had two gifts from God which Moses coveted: mercy and knowledge. Moses was told by Khadir never to question him about his actions. Moses failed to keep silence when Khadir performed three outwardly antisocial or baffling events: he had scuttled a boat; slain a young man without apparent provocation; and mended a falling wall belonging to people who had refused them hospitality. So Khadir left him, after explaining the hidden reasons for his actions: the boat was (temporarily) scuttled so that it would not be commandeered by an unscrupulous king; the young man would have become unfaithful to God; the wall had buried treasure beneath it, which it was seemly to keep from the vindictive townspeople. The point of the quranic story of Khadir is that God's actions only seem repulsive or outlandish to human beings; he knows things that humans do not. Perhaps Rumi was attempting to indicate to others that his relationship with Shams al-Din was a mystery known only to the two of them, and its strangeness to others was because outsiders did not know its import.

Shams al-Din either left Rumi suddenly, or else died *c*.1247. Later, Rumi found inspiration in a follower, Husam al-Din Hasan ibn

Muhammad. He called the *Mathnawi* 'the book of Husam'. It begins
with 'The Song of the Reed':

> Hearken to this Reed forlorn,
> Breathing ever since 'twas torn
> From its rushy bed, a strain
> Of impassioned love and pain.
>
> The secret of my song, though near,
> None can see and none can hear.
> O for a friend to show the sign
> And mingle all his soul with mine!
>
> 'Tis the flame of Love that fired me,
> 'Tis the wine of Love inspired me.
> Wouldst thou hear how lovers bleed,
> Hearken, hearken to the Reed!
> (Nicholson (trans.), *Rúmí: Poet and Mystic*, 31)

There are echoes in this poem of the first quranic revelation that
God 'taught humanity by the pen that which he did not know'
(Q96.4f.). Yet the language of Rumi's works, though redolent with
quranic allusions and devotion to Muhammad, underwent
idiosyncratic metamorphoses. Indeed, this poem underscores just
how subversive Rumi's works seem to Muslims who practise non-
Sufi ways of faith. The Persian reed-flute has always been
associated with members of the *mawlawiyya* order, for whom
music and dancing, which many Sunni Muslims forbid or frown
upon, are prominent features. Moreover the passage's erotic,
probably homoerotic, analogy of divine and human all-embracing
love is anathema to many Muslims: Rumi likened himself to a
flute on the lips of Husam, pouring forth 'the wailful music that
he made'. Certainly, homosexuality is forbidden by the Quran
(Q7.80f.). Another insight into Rumi's description of his intimate
relationship with Husam is to draw a parallel with Muhammad's
reception of revelation and his deep familiarity with God: Rumi's
rapport with Husam mirrors God's inbreathing his Prophet with
the Quran.

Rumi depicts Sufi leaders as the 'light of the Prophet'. This is a
large claim, but not exactly *bida*, since it does not detract from
Muhammad's status as the last prophet. Thus Rumi's work is both
profoundly rooted in love for Muhammad and the Quran, yet

deeply disloyal to its meaning as many other Muslims would conceive it.

However, much of Rumi's thought is grounded in Islamic orthodoxy. For example, he condemned asceticism as practised by Christian hermits (the Quran disapproves of monasticism, Q57.27). Moreover, comparing himself with a Sufi of a much earlier period, al-Hallaj, who was executed in Baghdad in 922 for apparently claiming too close an identity with God, Rumi maintained that he 'has not spoken and will not speak words of infidelity: do not disbelieve him'. He was, however, outspoken in his condemnation of Sunni Muslim scholars who, in his opinion, overestimated God's determination of events. He told the story of a man who climbed a tree and ate the fruit. When this pilferer was caught, he explained to the gardener that it was God's garden, and he was eating God's fruit given by him. Whereupon, the gardener trounced him 'with the stick of God given by him', until the robber conceded that the wrongdoing was of his own will, not a result of God's compulsion. Rumi's is an amusing mockery of the sterile arguments into which he believed much Islamic *kalam* (scholastic theology) had fallen.

Muhammad *in* Popular Islam

A Muslim's life of prayer and devotion does not rest simply upon the five daily prayers required of him or her. Nor need devotees of the Prophet be spiritual athletes, like many Sufis. Popular Islam provides ways in which ordinary Muslims can express their devotion to the Prophet.

The rites of passage in Islam are based on quranic words and prophetic practice, and provide illustrations of the importance of the Prophet's teaching and practices for ordinary Muslims through the ages. The institution of marriage is considered in chapter 4; here, we shall briefly consider ceremonies relating to a Muslim's birth and death. As soon as possible after birth, the *shahada* is whispered, often by the father, first into the child's right ear, then, in a slightly different form, in the left. In its minimal form it consists of the words 'There is no god but God and Muhammad is his messenger', but a more elaborate version is often used on this occasion. So the first ritually prescribed words a baby hears are an extended account of the central utterance of Muslim faith. Seven days after birth, the *aqiqa* ceremony takes place, when the baby's head is shaved. On such occasions, Muhammad would sometimes place a date in the baby's mouth, which he had first chewed into a pulp. This reminded others of the 'sweetness' of a newborn child. At this ceremony, the child is also named. Lots of boys are named after the Prophet, either in Arabic or another local language. Muslims boys are circumcised, either at the *aqiqa* ceremony or at any time thereafter until they are thirteen years old. Circumcision indicates that Muslims inherit the promises given by God to Abraham and other prophets in the Semitic, monotheistic tradition of faith. Some Muslim stories recount that Muhammad and other prophets were born already circumcised. Muslims believe that, at birth, all human beings are naturally *muslim*, at peace with and submissive to God; so any convert is really better described as a re-vert. A new Muslim will often be invited to recite the *shahada* before witnesses.

Muslim beliefs about death and judgement, as well as about birth, are strongly shaped by the teaching and traditions of the Prophet. Pre-Islamic Arabian religion was sceptical about an afterlife. However, the Muslim belief is that 'No soul shall die but by God's permission, according to what is written' (Q3.145). When a person is dying, friends and relatives will gather and recite the *shahada*, so that the last words he or she hears in this life are the name of God and his Prophet, just as were heard at the entrance to life. The funeral rites often include blessings invoked on Muhammad and descendants. Muslims are always buried, never cremated, and when the corpse is lowered into the earth, a common prayer is: 'We commit you to the ground in the name of God and in the religion of the Prophet'.

Some of the byways of popular Islam may be condemned or looked down upon by many of their practitioners' more austere or fastidious co-religionists. One controversial practice is the use of prayer-beads (*subha*). Some mystics refuse to use them, on the grounds that worshippers should be lost in prayer, not distracted by the mechanics of counting beads. The Wahhabis, followers of the strict teachings of Ibn Abd al-Wahhab (1703–92) of the Hanbali school of Muslim law, regard the *subha* as a needless and worthless superstition. Ordinary Muslims, though, often use them in informal prayer. A full Islamic rosary consists of ninety-nine beads, each indicating the ninety-nine names of God. These 'most beautiful names' (*al-asma al-husna*), an Arabic phrase found in the Quran (e.g. Q7.180), are found mostly in the Quran, though some come from the *hadith*. Some of the most important are: *al-rahman, al-rahim,* 'gracious, merciful'; *al-awwal, al-akhir,* 'the first and the last'; *al-qaiyum,* 'the self-subsisting'; and so on. It is characteristic of popular Islam, following the teaching and practice of the Prophet, that God is rarely the subject of detailed theological scrutiny, but is instead described epigrammatically and even elusively. The number, ninety-nine, hints at humankind's incomplete knowledge of God: more names could be added from scripture and traditions, but no Muslim ever contemplates the hundredth name. That incompleteness witnesses to a God who is beyond our reach: 'He reveals nothing of himself save what he wills' (Q2.255). There is a proverb that the superior smile on the face of a camel is because he alone knows the hundredth name!

The name of God is often on the lips of Muslims. When a person sneezes, bystanders declare, in Arabic, 'Praise be to God', words from the opening *sura* of the Quran. Perhaps the most common pious expression is *in shaa-Llah,* 'if God wills', after any statement of intent. To be sure, habitual piety can become merely formalized and meaningless. But it need not. One of the best illustrations of Muhammad's continuing and central importance to a billion of the world's inhabitants is that way in which the everyday language of Muslims is full of references to the God whom he revealed, in the words and language of the scripture he brought. In Muslims' houses, and in mosques, there are often pictures, plaques or rugs in which, in the language of Islam, the name of Muhammad is entwined with that of God.

Many Muslim men visit mosques, and, indeed, should do so for communal midday Friday prayers. (In many parts of the Muslim world, women rarely, if ever, visit the mosque. They say prayers at home. There are moves afoot among Muslim modernizers to change this practice and to encourage women to return to the mosque. After all, they point out, Muhammad's wives lived in the first mosque ever built.) Like Muhammad's in Madina, mosques fulfil many roles. The widespread conjoining of God's name with Muhammad's on mosque walls indicates that God loves his Prophet and those who follow and reverence him. These buildings often make significant use of space and light, with spacious courtyards which symbolically proclaim that God cannot be contained within the confines of any edifice, however hallowed.

There are also other specific sacred spaces. A popular practice in much of the Muslim world, not least South Asia, is devotion to and intercession at the shrines of holy people. These are memorials to someone who has become so close to God as to be able to intercede on behalf of those who turn to him (very occasionally, her) in prayer. Muslims flock to such tombs, where they perform ritual and private petitionary prayers. They may tie ribbons to trees, and ask for their heart's desire: health, the birth of a child, prosperity. They listen to religious songs, performed by musicians or, these days, on tapes or compact discs over loudspeakers. Such a 'saint' is often known by the Persian word, *pir*. *Pirs* may have been dead for many years, or may be alive and well. Even if they are dead, their devotees will talk as if they are alive and powerful. The Quran appears to forbid intercession (e.g. Q2.254, 6.51), yet part of the famous 'Throne Verse' (Q2.255) seems to suggest that intercession may exist by God's permission. The veneration of *pirs* often happens in areas where Muhammad himself is deeply reverenced, particularly for his intercessory powers on behalf of believers.

Indeed, throughout much of the Muslim world, Muhammad functions for the masses as intercessor on Judgement Day. He was sent as 'mercy for the worlds' (Q21.107). He has been compared to the cloud that sends life-giving rain to the fields, bringing life to the dead earth. Some villagers in Turkey and Iran call the rain *rahmat*, 'mercy'. Many holy men possess *baraka*, the power of blessing, but the Prophet's name does so superlatively.

Such devotional practices can verge on the superstitious. Some people or institutions claim to possess a relic of the Prophet: a hair from his head or beard; his cloak; a woollen sheet he used. Many Muslims condemn such things, which they regard as misguided. But popular Islam is deeply woven into local structures of belief, and into social and religious practices in much of the Muslim world.

The rift between Sunni, Shia and Sufi Muslims, and the many who follow a sort of popular Islam, can be overemphasized. All are devoted to the Prophet Muhammad, yet many are the ways in which they interpret him and his role in constructing their variant forms of being Islamic. Many Muslims believe that Muhammad prophesied that his followers would become divided:

'My people will experience what the Bani Israil [Children of Israel] experienced, as closely as one sandal represents another . . . The Bani Israil divided into 72 sects, but my people will divide into 73 sects, all of which but one will go to hell.' On being asked which it was, he replied, 'It is the one to which I and my companions belong.' (Robson, *Mishkat al-masabih*, 45)

This pessimistic and probably fabricated narrative reflects the gloom of a later generation of Muslims about Islam's failure to provide the unity of response that God requires of his people. Muslims, they believed, had failed God even more than the Jews. This raises the questions: what does Islam provide that other religious communities cannot or do not? And how much diversity is permitted and even desirable in the modern world, not only within Islam but in other religious and ideological communities?

Muhammad *and* Other World Faiths

M any conflicts in the contemporary world have a strong religious component. The attitude of each religion towards other faiths and ideologies is therefore an important issue. This chapter describes what the Quran or the Prophet himself had to say about relations with Christians and Jews, then examines the defensive attitudes and actions Muslims have taken towards other religions. After that it examines why Muslims and Christians share a history of mutual suspicion and looks at quranic and later Muslim attitudes to Jesus.

Muhammad, Jews *and* Christians

The quranic attitude towards other faiths was largely shaped by the context of paganism in which Muhammad lived. God and his Prophet denounced it. Yet there was also a history of monotheism in Arabia. Muhammad's practical experience of it was mainly through Jewish tribes.

In Madina, Muhammad hoped that the Madinan Jews would support him and his message about the unity of God. At first, the Quran speaks favourably of them and other monotheistic groups:

> Believers, Jews, Christians and Sabaeans [possibly the Mandaeans of
> Southern Iraq], whoever believes in God and the last day, and does
> what is right, will have a reward from their Lord (Q2.62)

Muhammad's hopes were dashed. When it became clear that the Jews
rejected his prophetic claims, he distanced himself from them. At first
the Muslims in Madina (or maybe just the *ansar* among them) prayed
towards Jerusalem and fasted on the Day of Atonement. Then,
Muhammad received the revelation that Abraham had built the Kaba
(Q2.124–7), and that he was not a Jew or a Christian; his religion was
Islam (Q2.128–41). Muslims were commanded henceforth to pray in
the direction of the Kaba (Q2.124–50), and, a little later, the Muslim
fast of Ramadan was instituted ((Q2.185–7). In due course, as
Muhammad vanquished his enemies, he marginalized and then
expelled three Jewish tribes. The third, the Banu Qurayza, suffered
bloody punishment (see chapter 1, pp. 25–6).

The Quran calls Jews and Christians 'People of the Book', *ahl al-
kitab*, because they possess a scripture. Quranic references to *ahl al-
kitab* are partly hostile, because Jews and Christians have misread and
disobeyed their scripture; and partly friendly, exhorting them to restore
the pristine purity of their faith and to join battle with Muslims against
infidelity and irreligion. The Quran also addresses the Banu Israil, the
'Children of Israel', who are reminded that they were called by God
and have forgotten this privilege. When the Quran addresses the
yahud, 'Jews', this refers mainly to those Jews who opposed
Muhammad's work in Madina. A case can therefore be made that it
was never Muhammad's or the Quran's intention to condemn all Jews
utterly. Rather, the emphasis is upon summoning Jews back to an
obedience to God from which they had fallen short.

Many Muslims, during the Prophet's lifetime and since, have
recognized this. Muslim relations with Jews have not always been
based on the stern treatment of some Madinan Jews by the Prophet of
Islam. Rather, they have often followed more positive quranic
references to the Jews. Jews had no homeland until the creation of the
state of Israel in 1948; they lived scattered and powerless except where,
very occasionally, a local ruler granted them limited authority and
autonomy. For much of the Middle Ages, Jews were treated much
better in Muslim than in Christian lands. In the latter, they were

sometimes persecuted as 'Christ-killers', yet many of them held high and honoured positions in Baghdad, the cities of Muslim Spain, and elsewhere. This can be overstated. Muslims did occasionally persecute Jews, and Jews could live peacefully in some Christian lands. But, by and large, Muslims have acted honourably towards Jews who lived in their territories. Today, there is great tension between Israel and many Islamic countries, and a consequent anti-Semitism or at least anti-Zionism prevalent among many Muslims. These should not obscure what has often been a mutually profitable history of relations between Jews and Muslims.

Because Madinan Jews rejected his prophetic claims, Muhammad's religion quickly came to have its own sense of identity in Madina, separate from Judaism, and also Christianity. Muhammad probably had fewer relations with Christians and less knowledge of their religion. A verse revealed in the early days in Madina commends them but not the Jews:

> You [Muhammad] will find that Jews and idolaters are most hostile towards the believers whereas the closest in love to the believers are those who say 'We are Christians.' (Q5.82)

But such approval did not last. Muhammad's rift with the Jews and Christians of Madina was one factor in the formulation of a specifically Arabian monotheistic tradition, associated with Abraham (see chapter 2, pp. 32–3). This was self-consciously set against Judaism and Christianity: 'Abraham was neither a Jew nor a Christian, but he was true in faith, and bowed his will to God's, and he was not an idolater' (Q3.67). This new reformed Arabian monotheism had universal aspirations. The Quran says:

> We [God] have made you [Muslims] a moderate community so that you may be witnesses for humankind, just as the Messenger is a witness for you. (Q2.143)

Muslims have interpreted 'moderate' to mean that Islam was created to avoid the extravagances or excesses of other communities. For example, the food laws in Islam mark a middle way between the extreme formalism of Jewish regulations (which the Quran sees as an imposition upon Jews for the sin of keeping many from God's path, Q4.160), and the lack of any in Christianity.

Muhammad quickly came to see that he could expect no genuine alliance with other monotheistic groups, a view confirmed by the Quran:

> Believers! Do not take the Jews and the Christians as your allies: they are allies only of each other. Whoever among you becomes a friend to them is one of them. God does not guide unrighteous people. (Q5.51)

Although the quranic disapproval of the Madinan Jews and Christians stems mainly from their failure to support Muhammad's ministry, it is bolstered by their failure to uphold the unity of God:

> The Jews say 'Ezra is a son of God', and the Christians say 'Christ is a son of God'. That is a saying of their tongue which simply imitates what the unbelievers of old used to say. God's curse be on them: how astray they are! (Q9.30)

This rather curious accusation against Ezra may reflect his key role in the renewal of Judaism after the Babylonian exile. Actually, mainstream Jews would not grant him the divine status Christians accord Jesus. The Quran is not absolutely clear about the fate of these aberrant monotheistic precursors of Islam. Post-quranic scholarship created seven ranks of hell, based on an imaginative, and arguably uncharitable and false, exegesis of quranic passages. *Laza*, a word found only once in the Quran, is a blazing fire for Christians. *Al-hutama*, found twice, is a kindled fire for Jews. A more straightforward reading of the Quran does not support these uncharitable interpretations of those words. However, the Quran does state that, 'If anyone desires another religion than Islam, it will never be accepted from him, and on the last day he will be among the losers' (Q3.85). Some Muslim modernists quote against this, 'There must be no compulsion in religion' (Q2.256), but the two verses are not addressing the same issue. To maintain that people should not be forced to believe something is not to agree that whatever they believe is right and that God will accept it from them.

In Q3.85 the word 'Islam' could mean 'submission'. If so, then Christians, Jews and others could claim to submit to God, though in their own religious *umma*s, not in the *umma* of Islam. This possible translation has not been followed by many Muslims. Yet it may have force in it. The Quran condemns Madinan Jews and Christians for never being satisfied until people follow their form of religion (Q2.120). It may therefore be inconsistent if it insists that the community of Islam alone is the way to God. Some Muslims have justified a hardline interpretation on the grounds that Islam alone has kept its revelation pure and undefiled, yet this seems a sentimental, optimistic reading of Islamic history, denied by much internal as well as external evidence. Indeed, the Quran itself recognizes that different communities of faith will continue to exist:

> To you we sent the true scripture, confirming the scriptures that came before it, and preserving them. So judge between them by what God has revealed, and do not follow their whims, diverging from the truth that has come to you. To each of you we have given a law and an open way. If God had so willed, he would have made you a single people, but instead he tests you by what he has given you. So strive to excel in good deeds. Finally, you will all return to him, and he will show you the truth of the matters in which you were at variance. (Q5.48)

Here, the criterion of acceptability is godly deeds rather than perfect conformity to theological or legal beliefs and practices. Muslims are confident that Islam's moderation in creeds and deeds gives them an advantage over other monotheistic groups.

So, in contrast to the imperfect monotheism of Judaism and Christianity, Islam came into being as a godly community, worshipping the one God who is the object of a person's deepest commitment. In the Quran, the Prophet was instructed to say:

> My prayer and service, my living and dying, belong to God, lord of all creation. He has no partner: with that [message] I am commanded, and I am the first Muslim. (Q6.162)

Elsewhere the Quran says:

> God witnesses that there is no god save he, as do the angels, and people who have [revealed] knowledge and uphold justice. There is no god but he, the almighty, the wise. The true religion with God is Islam. (Q3.18)

These verses display a certain ambiguity. As the word 'Islam' can simply mean 'submission' or 'peace', the last part of Q3.18 could read 'The true religion with God is [to live in] peace.'

However, there are indications that by the end of Muhammad's life, God and the Prophet saw Islam as a distinct religion, self-consciously separate from Judaism and Christianity. This was the logic of the trend set in motion in the early Madinan years, when Muslims were forced to forge an identity distinct from, rather than alongside, other Arabian monotheists. It is illustrated by the occasion when, in February and March 632, Muhammad made the major pilgrimage (*hajj*) to Makka, as it had been prescribed to him by God. When the pilgrims met in the valley of Mina, he delivered 'The Speech from the White Camel' to the massed ranks of believers. During it came the revelation: 'This day I have perfected your religion for you, completed my favour towards you, and chosen for you Islam as your religion' (Q5.3). Most Muslims agree that this was the last quranic revelation. Muhammad also said to the enormous crowd: 'I have left among you God's book, the Quran. If you hold fast to it, you will not go astray. Have I fulfilled my mission?' All answered, 'You have fulfilled it, Messenger of God.' Muhammad lifted his eyes to heaven, and called out three times, 'God, you are witness. God, you are witness. God, you are witness.' He died in Madina three months later.

Muhammad: Defender *of the* Faith

In the view of most Muslims, by the end of the Prophet's life Islam was a distinct and perfected religion, revealing through its scripture the clear signs of God. Islam explains very clearly the need to obey God, and offers the means to do so through its framework of law. Hence, one reason why many Muslims are concerned with *jihad* (struggle) and *ridda* (apostasy) is because they believe that they are obliged to defend the last and final revelation of God. After all, Muhammad had had to defend it against Makkan persecution, the deviousness of the *munafiqun*, and the negative attitudes and actions of Jews and Christians he encountered.

The five pillars of Islam are: *shahada* (the profession of faith that 'There is no god but God, and Muhammad is his Prophet'); *salat* (ritual prayer); *zakat* (almsgiving); *sawm* (fasting during the month of Ramadan); and *hajj* (pilgrimage to Makka). Some minority groups in Islam regard *jihad* as the sixth *arkan al-din* (pillar of Islam). This is because it is very important to them that Islam, as the only completely committed and obedient community, should continue to exist. The Quran justifies *jihad* in this way:

> Struggle in the cause of God against those who fight you, but do not be aggressors, for God does not like aggressors. And slay them wherever you catch them, and turn them out from where they have turned you out; for oppression is worse than slaughter. Do not fight them at the Sacred Mosque, unless they fight you there; but if they fight you, slay them. This is the reward for unbelievers. But if they desist, God is forgiving and merciful. Fight them until there is no more subversion, and religion belongs to God. But if they desist, let there be no hostility except to those who practise oppression. (Q2.190–3)

This passage is about Muslims fighting the pagan Makkans, not about warring between believers. So when Muslim dictators call a *jihad* against another Muslim country, they abuse the concept. Similarly, because *jihad* is a defensive, not aggressive, act, hostage-taking in the name of *jihad* is a violation of its meaning.

For many Muslim scholars, overt violence, even in a godly cause, is the 'lesser *jihad*'. The more important 'greater *jihad*' is the individual's internal struggle to conform his or her will to God. Many base this on Q9.20:

> Those who believe and go into exile and struggle [*jihad*] in the cause of God with their property and own selves, have higher rank with God. They are achievers.

The quranic translator Yusuf Ali comments about this verse:

> Here is a good description of *Jihad*. It *may* require fighting in God's cause, as a form of self-sacrifice. But its essence consists in (1) a true and sincere Faith, which so fixes its gaze on God, that all selfish or worldly motives seem paltry and fade away, and (2) an earnest and ceaseless activity, involving the sacrifice (if need be) of life, person or property, in the service of God. Mere brutal fighting is opposed to the whole spirit of *Jihad*, while the sincere scholar's pen or preacher's voice or wealthy man's contribution may be the most valuable forms of *Jihad*. (Ali, *The Holy Quran: Text, Translation and Commentary*, n. 1270)

Still, Muslim jurists have recognized that *jihad* involves fighting others. They justify this in some detail; an interesting parallel could be made with Christian theories of the just war.

The concept of *jihad* is related to the *dar al-Islam* ('the abode of Islam', regions which are subject to Islamic law) and the *dar al-harb* ('the abode of war', non-Islamic territories). There has been much controversial debate by Islamic scholars about the correlation between these two domains. Some scholars believe that it is the duty of Muslims to transform the latter into the former, by force if necessary. Syed Karamat Ali (1800–73), was one of many scholars who argued differently. Towards the end of his life, he wrote a justification of British rule in India. He was an adherent of the Hanafi school of jurisprudence and argued that the three conditions laid down by Abu Hanifa (d. 767) for the conversion of a *dar al-Islam* into a *dar al-harb* were not satisfied. Karamat Ali contended that most of the rulings of Islam in the sphere of marriage, divorce, dower and inheritance were in force under British rule; that Muslims enjoyed full religious freedom; and that countries next to India (to the north-west) were Muslim. He wrote after the Indian Uprising of 1857, which finally ended theoretical Muslim rule in the subcontinent (in practice, British rule had replaced the Mughal dynasty's authority long before). Thus, his was a retrospective justification. It was also a realistic recognition of the political *status quo* in his time. This does not make it a piece of cynical scholarship. Most Muslims recognize the need to live at peace with their neighbours, except when their religion is thereby endangered. Zealots, hardliners or 'fundamentalists' in every religion may make headline news, but they do not always, or even usually, represent the heart of the religion, or the mind of that faith's founder.

Many Muslims believe that apostasy is a particularly reprehensible crime. One reason is that, if someone has been shown God's clear signs but then rejects them, he or she is then in manifest and perverse error. Another is psychological: a member who leaves has a distressing effect upon a community which strives in the way of God to do his will. The Quran prescribes punishment for a *murtadd* (one who turns back), not on earth but only in the life to come. There, apostates will earn a 'dreadful penalty' (Q16.106). However, many *hadith* introduce the death penalty in this life for renegades. For example, according to a *hadith* traced to his wife Aisha, Muhammad permitted that anyone 'who abandons religion and separates himself from the community' should be killed.

If many of the Prophet's earliest followers in Makka had fallen back into paganism, the community would have been hard pressed to survive. Later, in Madina, the *munafiqun* worked to destroy Islam (Q63.1–8). These 'hypocrites' did not mean what they said when they affirmed that God was one and that Muhammad was his Prophet. It is therefore understandable that apostasy was then a nefarious crime. However, many Muslims are embarrassed when, these days, their co-religionists frame apostasy laws, prescribing death as the penalty, to prevent Muslims leaving Islam. Liberal Muslims argue that the situation is quite different now, compared to what it was in the Prophet's lifetime.

Apostasy is an outstanding example of the tension in Islam between individual responsibility and choice, and communal identity. Individual Muslims differ in their practical commitment to the laws of Islam, so that (for example) some will pray all the required daily prayers, while others will pray occasionally and some not at all. But few contemplate publicly withdrawing from their religion. One reason is that Islam is not just a focus for people's personal faith. It is a community which, theoretically at least, governs the whole of life of the divine society; educational, economic, social and political. The unity of the divine society reflects the unity of God.

In practice, Muslims have always been able to find a role for *ahl al-kitab*, 'People of the Book', those who have a scripture which reveals God as one, especially Jews, Christians and Zoroastrians. Medieval Islam imposed a poll tax (*jizya*) on non-Muslims who were *ahl al-kitab*, justifying it on the basis of Q9.29:

> Fight the People of the Book who do not believe in God or the last day, or do not forbid what God and his messenger forbid, and do not acknowledge the religion of truth, until they pay the *jizya* with willing submission, and feel themselves subdued.

The *jizya* permitted Christians, Jews and other monotheists in Muslim-majority lands to worship God in their own ways. It also exempted them from military service. However, the *jizya* sometimes operated as a more general tax. From time to time, Muslim rulers levied it on non-monotheistic subjects. Occasionally they did not impose it at all.

Some modernists have included Hinduism, Buddhism and other non-monotheistic theological and philosophical traditions as, to some extent, revealed by God. For example, Ameer Ali included Jesus, Moses, Zoroaster, the Buddha and Plato among those whose work was completed by Muhammad (Ali, *The Spirit of Islam*, 111).

Because Islam is considered to be the last and final religion, and Muhammad the 'seal of the prophets', Muslims find it difficult to integrate post-Islamic religions, and especially (in their view) heterodox Islamic movements like the Ahmadiyya and the Bahais into any scheme that values other religions. The Ahmadiyya movement was founded in 1889 by Mirza Ghulam Ahmad (*c.*1839–1908), who made several important claims about himself: he was an *avatara* of the Hindu god Krishna; the *mahdi* (the rightly guided one); and the messiah. The Ahmadiyya have split into two groups. From a Muslim point of view, the Qadiyanis, who believe that Ghulam Ahmad was a *nabi* (prophet) are clearly heretical, the Lahoris, who believe him to have been a *mujaddid* (renewer), less explicitly so. The Bahai religion arose within the milieu of Iranian Islam. Its founder, Bahaullah (1817–92) is regarded by Bahais as a prophet, as is his forerunner, Mirza Ali Muhammad (1819–50), the *bab* or 'door'.

Some Muslims persecute both movements, even today, often for political and economic, as much as religious, reasons, but this is not the whole picture. Some Muslims work for the common good even with post-Islamic religions. In the United Kingdom the Inter-Faith Network is a national organization that includes Muslims, Sikhs and Bahais (though not as yet Ahmadiyyas) among its member-organizations. In India and elsewhere, some Muslim and Sikh mystics and visionaries sit at each other's feet to learn from and pray with one another. In Pakistan, although the Ahmadiyyas have been marginalized and even persecuted by government legislation in recent years, many held high office in the early years after independence. Yusuf Ali's English translation of the Quran is still widely read by many Muslims; he was an Ahmadi.

Muhammad: Successful Political Leader

Islam is regarded by many outsiders as a warrior faith, ruthlessly antagonistic towards other creeds. Many non-Muslims, particularly Christians, believe that Muhammad was the originator of a belligerent religion, conquering with a Quran in one hand and a scimitar in the other.

This distorted interpretation arose from the fact that Muhammad was a more successful political leader than any other human founder of a world religion. Before Moses died, he had obeyed God and appointed Joshua to lead the Jews into the Promised Land. They took possession of the region from other groups but, except in the heyday of King David and King Solomon, always held it insecurely.

Jesus did not try to wrest political control of his country from the Romans. Some of his followers may have wanted him to, but, if so, he ignored them. For the first four centuries of Christian history, his followers were members of an often marginalized and persecuted religious sect. Only under the reign of the Emperor Constantine (306–37) did Christianity become the state religion of the Roman Empire.

By contrast, Muhammad needed no Joshua or Constantine. He was the political and religious leader of a community which, upon his death, controlled most of Arabia and was poised to spread further abroad. In 732, exactly one century after Muhammad's death, Charles Martel repulsed Muslim invaders in what is now south-west France, at the Battle of Poitiers. Well before then, the Eastern Roman Empire had been reduced to a shadow of its former self: Jerusalem fell to the Arab armies in 637, and the Christian heartlands of North Africa also succumbed. Muslims entered Spain. Were it not for that victory at Poitiers, most Western Europeans would now, perhaps, be Muslims. Eventually, due in no small measure to the unwillingness of the Western Church to support the Orthodox Emperor of Byzantium, Constantinople fell to the Muslim Ottoman Turks in 1453. The Balkans came under Ottoman rule. As late as 1683, the Turks laid siege to the gates of Vienna. One result of the Ottoman presence was the conversion of some Christians to Islam: the legacy in Bosnia is apparent in the contemporary world, appallingly.

For well over a thousand years, a dread of Islam gripped the European imagination. From a Christian perspective, the threat was a real one. Europe could have become part of the Islamic *umma*. All sorts of tales grew up about the evils of that religion and its Prophet. One story told how Muhammad was a cardinal who, despite lavish bribes, failed to be elected as pope and so, in a fit of pique, started his own religion. This reflects a persistent but grotesquely untrue Christian conviction that Islam is, at bottom, the ultimate Christian heresy. In the medieval Christian perception, Islam distorted pure doctrine and threatened to sweep true faith away. The Muslim threat has a far longer ancestry in Europe than 'the yellow peril' or 'Reds under the bed'. Small wonder, then, that with the breakdown of the Soviet Empire, Muslims have again become the West's major ideological 'enemy'.

Yet two considerations must be placed alongside this history of fear and misrepresentation. The first is that Islam and the Christian West have not been hermetically sealed from each other. There have always been links between them. The English Queen Elizabeth I (d. 1603) appealed to a Turkish Sultan to join forces with her against Spain, on the grounds of their shared faith in one God. More humane and positive, though, than political posturing have been intellectual links. In particular, medieval Spain provided mutual intellectual stimulation. Muslims rediscovered Greek philosophy, medicine and other disciplines. They translated them into Arabic and refracted them through minds shaped by a belief in the unity of all knowledge, reflecting the unity of God. Then they gave them back to Christian European thinkers. The influence of Muslim thinkers upon the great Christian theologian Thomas Aquinas (1226–74) was considerable. Works of Aristotle were among those which had been preserved by Muslims in Arabic translations. Aquinas gave a systematic and rational account of Christian doctrine based heavily on Aristotelian science and philosophy, some of which had been filtered through the sensibilities of Muslims like Ibn Rushd (known in Christian Europe as Averroes; 1126–98). Without Muslim reverence for, and preservation of, past learning, Aquinas could not have made this synthesis. Sadly, this did not stop him from condemning aspects of Islam that he imperfectly understood.

The second consideration is that Christian fears and misrepresentations of Islam, yet indebtedness to it, operate vice versa. In 1076, Pope Gregory VII wrote to the Muslim ruler of what is now Algeria:

> Almighty God approves nothing in us so much as that, after loving God, one should love his fellow man. You and we owe this charity to ourselves because we believe in, and confess, one God, admittedly in a different way. (Daniel, *Islam and the West*, 64)

Yet less than twenty years later, his successor Pope Urban II launched the First Crusade. The Crusades took place, on and off, until the end of the thirteenth century. This long history of religious superstition and idealism, larded with political and economic factors and human wickedness, has gone deep into the Muslim (and also the Jewish) psyche. Christians are seen as looters, rapists and criminals, who seek a religious sanction for their human shortcomings.

Muslim fears of Christian violence and exploitation have increased in modern times. For much of the nineteenth and twentieth centuries, Muslims lived under the sway of British, Dutch or French rulers, who were perceived as Christian even though some of their actions were not modelled on the Prince of Peace they claimed to venerate. Despite the recent economic power of many Muslim countries because of petrodollars, Western political dominance has largely been replaced by economic supremacy, particularly that of the USA. Fear and mistrust breeds misrepresentation. When Iranians called America 'the great Satan', this may cause Westerners to laugh and scoff. Instead, they should recognize the judgement of many Muslims that the political leader of the Western world is overweeningly arrogant, devious and contemptuous of God's will. So is the rest of what is, in the Muslim view, the technologically advanced but emotionally and religiously underdeveloped West.

Yet there has been fruitful interchange for Muslims with Christians. Much of the Sufi way has been heavily dependent upon Christian thought and practice, though poured into Muslim moulds. Even today, Muslims appropriate Western, perhaps 'Christian', education, medicine and technology (just as Christians borrowed similar Muslim achievements in the Middle Ages). The presence of perhaps one million Muslims in the United Kingdom today (and even greater numbers in Germany and France) has arisen to a large extent from their desire for economic betterment.

Muhammad *and* Jesus

In his prophetic ministry, Muhammad was far more involved with Jews than with Christians. Moreover, in its beliefs and practices, Islam is much closer to Judaism than to Christianity. Yet the course of history has brought Muslims and Christians together, often for evil rather than for good. Today, in a nuclear age, but also for the more positive reason that both believe they witness to the presence of a merciful transcendent reality, it is important for them to relate positively to each other. Because Muhammad had less contact with Christians in Madina than with Jews, his primary disagreements with them were possibly more theoretical and lay elsewhere, in the realm of theology.

The Quran's chief complaints against Christianity are its claim that Jesus is the Son of God, and the doctrine of the Trinity. At first glance, this seems strange. Islam is much more interested in obeying the revealed will of God than in contemplation of doctrine. Although some scholars have thought that Muhammad chided Christians precisely because of their obsession with the intellectual niceties of their faith rather than its ethical and social demands, this is to miss the point. As Muhammad saw it, the Christian concept of God struck at the heart of his prophetic vision of the monotheistic community. Was he right so to interpret it? It will help us, first of all, to examine the quranic evidence about the death of Jesus and then Christian Trinitarian beliefs.

The death of Jesus has been a particularly important area of dispute between orthodox Muslims and Christians. An examination of its quranic explanation will help us understand why. Most Muslims interpret *sura* Q4.155–8 as a denial of the crucifixion:

> So for breaking their [the Jews'] covenant, and disbelieving the signs of God, and killing the prophets without right, . . . and for their unbelief, and their speaking against Mary a great slander; and for their saying: 'We killed the Messiah, Jesus the Son of Mary, the messenger of God' – though they did not kill him, and did not crucify him, but only a likeness of it was shown to them. Truly, those who have gone in different ways about him are in doubt about him; they have no knowledge of him and only follow speculation; though they certainly did not kill him. No, to be sure, God raised him to himself. God is almighty and wise. And there is no People of the Book but will surely believe in him before his death, and on the day of resurrection he will be a witness against them.

The almost universally held view among Muslims about this passage is that the Jews tried to kill Jesus but were unable to do so. This raises two important questions: did Jesus really die on the cross? Was there a substitute who suffered in his place? The canonical gospels affirm the first and have no suggestion of the second. Many Muslims, however, deny the first and affirm the second; they have some support in the teaching of the second-century CE Egyptian gnostic and Christian, Basilides, whose views only survive in rather diverse interpretations by his opponents. The idea of a substitute, perhaps Judas Iscariot or Simon of Cyrene, has been accepted by some notable Muslim commentators of the Quran. For example, Tabari believed that a Jewish chief called Joshua, to whom God gave the form and appearance of Jesus, died in his place. (Perhaps Tabari was unaware that Joshua and Jesus are variant forms of the same name in Hebrew.) However, the passage hardly demands this interpretation, which does not seem its obvious import. The Arabic *shubbiha la-hum* is rendered by me into English as 'only a likeness of it was shown to them'. It is very possible that the Arabic words mentioned should be attached to the crucifixion and not to Jesus. Then the meaning of a very difficult passage could be that the Jews did not kill Jesus, rather than that he did not die.

It remains, however, a controversial and opaque passage. The Indian modernist, Sir Sayyid Ahmad Khan (1817–98), believed that after three or four hours Jesus was taken down from the cross by the disciples and kept in a secret place, for fear of the Jews. This resonates with the Ahmadiyya view that Jesus eventually went to Kashmir and died there.

Another view has been expressed by the Egyptian surgeon and educationalist, Kamel Hussein. In his book, translated into English by Kenneth Cragg as *City of Wrong*, he focused on the events leading to Good Friday.[1] Kamel Hussein's is a sensitive and moving account of the influence of Jesus upon a number of the participants involved in his arrest and condemnation, whether they be (to use the titles of three sections of the book) 'In Jewry', 'With the Disciples', or 'Among the Romans'. Yet in the final section, 'Golgotha and After', the author reaffirmed the traditional Islamic belief that Jesus was not crucified. One of his characters, the Wise Man, observes:

> There is one thing about the events of this day of which I am aware which you do not know. It is that God has raised the Lord Christ to Himself. He was the light of God upon the earth. The people of Jerusalem would have nothing to do with him except to extinguish the light. Whereupon God has darkened the world around them. This darkness is a sign from God to show that God has forbidden them the light of faith and the guidance of conscience. (Hussein, *City of Wrong*, 183)

This glosses over the central Christian belief that Jesus died. The author had informed his translator that

> No cultured Muslim believes . . . nowadays [that someone substituted for Jesus on the cross]. The text is taken to mean that the Jews thought they killed Christ but God raised him unto Him in a way we can leave unexplained among the several mysteries which we have taken for granted on faith alone. (Ibid., 222)

Geoffrey Parrinder has observed 'the significance of the cross Dr

1. This important work was first published in English in 1959 as *City of Wrong*, trans. Kenneth Cragg (London, Godfrey Bles); reprinted Oneworld (Oxford, 1994). Page references are to the 1959 edition.

Hussein sees to be in that men did crucify Jesus in intention, all their actions were bent towards it, and they utterly rejected the Christ of God' (Parrinder, *Jesus in the Quran*, 114). Maybe so, but Christian theology has, in its own estimation, been built upon more than an intention. It has been based, to some extent, upon the atoning death of Jesus, wrought upon the cross. However far Dr Hussein goes towards a Christian view of Good Friday, it is not far enough for many Christians.

It might be possible to attempt a different perspective on the quranic passage. This viewpoint would focus on the part that condemns the Jews for killing the prophets. Muhammad was aware that prophets were persecuted by communities to which they were sent. His life in Makka was a poignant illustration of this fact, yet he was convinced that the will of God should not and could not be thwarted by human disobedience. On this reading, the emphasis in this passage is not so much on whether or not Jesus actually died, as on the sheer wickedness of those Jews who worked to bring about the death of one of God's prophets. It is important to note that Muhammad believed that many, perhaps most, communities have attempted to silence their divine messenger. Jews are not singled out by the Quran as scapegoats, but as examples of the unwillingness of most human communities to receive and obey the message God sends them and its bearers: Muhammad, of course, had a particular awareness of the defects of the Madinan Jews in this regard.

The focus of this passage, then, is on the Jews' rejection of the message which the messenger brings, as paradigmatic of other communities' negative responses to God's revelation of his unity. There is no sense in these verses, or elsewhere in the Quran, of the identity of the message with the messenger, as Christians believe there is of the gospel with Jesus the Messiah, still less of an identification of Jesus with the person as well as the will of God. In this passage, as elsewhere in the Quran, Jesus fits into definitions and categories of what constitutes a prophet, as Islam, but not Christianity, interprets that concept. According to the Quran, he is a prophet to the Jews, bringing a scripture, and preaching the unity of God and the certainty of the Day of Judgement (Q3.42–63).

More important than the death of Jesus, because it is more certain what the Quran precisely means, is the revelatory material about the Trinity. This doctrine is regarded with particular horror: 'They are unbelievers who say that God is the Messiah, the son of Mary' (Q5.17). Of a certainty, in the quranic worldview:

> The Messiah, the son of Mary, was only a messenger. Many messengers died before him. His mother was sincere. They both ate food. (Q5.75, cf. Q5.72–7)

For the Quran and Muhammad, the doctrine of the Trinity strikes at the heart of the unity of God. Neither was interested in the subtleties of Christian reflections on this central Christian belief, which seeks to locate a pluralism of divine action and being within one Godhead. Although the Prophet of Islam, and its holy book, recognized the intention of Christians to be monotheists, and honoured that desire, they reckoned Christians as, in practice, polytheists or, more precisely, tri-theists:

> When God said, 'Jesus, son of Mary, have you told people, "Take me and my mother as two gods apart from God"?', he said, 'Glory be to you. It is not for me to say what I have no right to.' (Q5.116)

Thus, variant interpretations of God's unity clearly divide Muslims and Christians. Muslims believe Christians have diluted revealed monotheistic faith. Some Christians believe that Muslims are obsessed by a mathematical rather than relational interpretation of it.

What can be done about such an impasse? Any Christian who has talked with a Muslim about Jesus, and vice versa, will know how entrenched are the positions and how little scope there is for mutual understanding, still less agreement. A tentative way forward, then, may begin by aiming for understanding. Such an understanding would begin from recognizing that Islam and Christianity have developed into two quite different worldviews. Although they contain similar concepts (such as prophecy, and stories about common heroes), the resources for comparing them are quite different. So, for example, in the two religions, Jesus is a common figure, differently understood. Because Muslim perceptions of him differ from Christian ones, Christians believe that Muhammad was misinformed. Muslims, who are committed to a belief in the Quran as the pure word of God, hold that Christians must have distorted their sources and now have an imperfect remembrance of the ministry and meaning of Jesus.

It is easy for Christians and Muslims to regard the other's perceived shortcomings as sheer perversity. Rather, both justify their beliefs on quite different grounds. To be sure, these are important and irreconcilable differences. Christians believe that the quranic information shows that Muhammad was privy to inferior information from later sources than the New Testament, which confirms their conviction that the Quran is a human document. Muslims believe that Christians have disobeyed or at least watered down the central revelation given to them that God is one. Yet these differences are sincerely held. They are not due to culpable, wilful and perverse disobedience. To recognize this fact would be a great step forward, if more people were to take it. Already, some Christians argue that the Quran is divinely inspired, in the sense that God inspired many of the words and deeds of Muhammad. Also, many Muslims feel that Christians are sincere if misguided believers, and follow echoes of their pristine monotheistic revelation.

In practice, Jesus, although a figure greatly honoured by Muslims, is not centrally important in the construction of Islam's self-identity (except, perhaps, in parts of its mystical, Sufi tradition). Many Christian writers on aspects of Jesus in the Quran, by overestimating his importance to Islam, perpetuate the mistaken apprehension that Christian relations with Muslims can be built upon the shared figure of Jesus. In his book *Jesus in the Quran*, Parrinder noted some important facts about the quranic views of Jesus, which show his importance to Muslims:

> The Quran gives a greater number of honourable titles to Jesus than to any other figure of the past . . . Three chapters or suras of the Quran are named after references to Jesus (3, 5 and 19); he is mentioned in fifteen suras and ninety-three verses. (Parrinder, *Jesus in the Quran*, 16)

However, this evidence could be looked at from a different perspective. In particular, over six thousand verses of the Quran do not mention Jesus. Certainly, he is greatly honoured, but Ibrahim (Abraham) and Musa (Moses) are more important quranic figures. The titles he is granted, such as Messiah, are filled with Muslim meaning, not Christian interpretation. Indeed, if all references to Jesus were deleted from the Quran, the religion of Islam would not be significantly different, save in some of its mystical forms.

It might just be possible, though very difficult, to attempt a more innovative and imaginative look at quranic information and Christian meaning than has usually been attempted. For example, the crucial passage on the crucifixion berates the Jews for disbelieving in the signs (*ayat*) of God. The concept of signs is important in the Quran: it describes itself as 'a book whose *ayat* have been made distinct' (Q41.3). It would be possible for Muslims and Christians together to explore the focus and meaning of these signs and eventually for Christians to explain that Jesus is for them God's clearest sign of his presence in the world. This would not dissolve the disagreements between Muslims and Christians but it might set the debate within a more fruitful and creative setting than has hitherto been attempted by many scholars.

However, core Christian and Muslim beliefs about Jesus are so different that it is difficult to believe that he could ever be other than a divisive figure. This is perhaps harder for Christians to accept than Muslims, because Jesus is central to their faith, and is seen in their scriptures as a decisive and unifying figure for all creation (e.g. Ephesians 1, Hebrews 1). Dogmatically and legally, he is of no importance to the centre of Muslim faith.

One deduction from this would be that each religion should cherish its own prophets and heroes and, for the sake of reverence, guard them from outside evaluations. Another would be that this is an impossible hope, and that the scrutiny of figures who claim universal significance by outsiders should be welcomed, so long as it is done respectfully as well as honestly. Such esteem nevertheless has to reckon with the fact that Christians and Muslims have very different understandings of prophecy and revelation. These lead to quite different assessments of the import of those figures for human understanding and commitment. However much outsiders may honour and respect the other's human founder, they cannot affirm what the believer confesses.

Islam: A Minority Religion

Muslims have always been more comfortable working with the instincts of a majority group. Because they understand Islam to be a monotheistic theocracy, this has political implications as well as significance for an individual's personal religious observation. The religious justification for Muslims acting as if they were a majority comes from a conviction that they are the practitioners of God's final and clearest revelation.

This is sometimes inappropriate and even counter-productive. Although Muslims form a majority of the population in more than forty countries, Islam is numerically probably the third-largest religion after Christianity and Buddhism in today's global village.

Muslims in the West rightly draw attention to the way in which 'Christians' treat them unfairly and in a racist manner. They properly ask for redress under the law. Yet they do not always demand reciprocal rights for Christians and others in countries where Muslims persecute them or treat them as second-class citizens. Furthermore, some of the ways in which Muslims seek a just outcome for their rightful aspirations are ill considered. For example, the self-styled Muslim Parliament in Britain suggests that its creators lack an understanding of the importance of Britain's democratic history. It seems to set up a rival to the elected authority. Such organizations can be the tools of self-appointed leaders who have little knowledge of Islamic history, still less of anyone else's. However, they also rely for support upon the instincts of a group of people who expect to possess political authority, and regret that they do not have it. (Obviously, this is not the only reason: economic powerlessness, racism and other factors are very important.)

This instinctive expectation depends upon reading history in a particular way, which affirms Islam's political triumphs but not its failures. Despite the judgements of some scholars, an acceptance of political failure does not come more naturally to Shia than to Sunni Muslims. Majority 'twelver' Shia Islam has been largely a history of political failure, yet its looks forward to the return of the hidden Imam, who went into occultation in 874. When he comes again, he will reverse that failure. Today, Iran, with its large Shia majority, provides the focus for a vision of their political and economic empowerment for many Muslims, not only Shias.

Indeed, a nostalgic emphasis upon past greatness by many Muslims often hopes for its return. Such Muslims still look back to a golden age of unity, interpreted through rose-coloured spectacles. This can be illustrated by the history of the caliphate, the institution that provided Sunni Muslims with a political leader who succeeded Muhammad in that capacity and guarded, though could not change or improve, his spiritual legacy. Despite the widely held view among Sunni Muslims that the period of the *rashidun* caliphs (632–61) was a golden age, three of the first four successors to Muhammad as political leader of the Islamic *umma* were murdered. Moreover, they were succeeded by a dynasty, the Umayyads (who ruled until 750), whose clan members (the Abd Shams clan of the Quraysh) had bitterly opposed the Prophet during his Makkan years. The father of the first caliph of this regime, Muawiya (d. 680), was Abu Sufyan, who had resisted Muhammad until 630. Muawiya justified his assumption of caliphal power on the grounds that Ali, by failing to act against the murderers of Uthman, Muawiya's kinsman, had forfeited his moral right to lead the nascent community. This seems a cynical excuse to justify the triumph of one clan within the Quraysh over that of Muhammad. Within a third of a century of the Prophet's death, leadership of the Muslim community had become a prize for the powerful and the unprincipled. Ironically, his most ardent foes had taken over control of his monotheistic, politico-religious community.

The conviction Sunni Muslims hold of a united monotheistic community, exercising temporal power and also imposing spiritual obligations on believers, forms a potent myth. Yet it remains a myth that has only partially been achieved. True, Muhammad's ministry broke clan and tribal loyalties in Arabia in favour of commitment to Islam. But the triumph of Muawiya and the Ummayad dynasty illustrates how skin deep such a loyalty was: clan allegiance remained an important and arguably dominating factor in early Islam.

The myth of a united and powerful single Muslim *umma* is challenged by the facts of history. For example, the Ottoman Sultans who ruled Turkey for six centuries until 1922 claimed that the caliphate was transferred to the Ottoman Sultan Selim by the Abbasid caliph in 1517. However, there had not been a universally acknowledged caliphate since the fall of Baghdad to the Mongols in 1258. Even before then, the Abbasid caliphs had for many years exerted only a shadowy, theoretical power over the Sunni Muslim world. (The Abbasids replaced the Ummayads as caliphs in 750. They were descended from Abbas, a merchant uncle of Muhammad. He fought against the Prophet at the Battle of Badr where he was taken prisoner. He was released and became a Muslim.) Some local Muslim rulers had acknowledged the universal caliphal authority of the Abbasids, but others had struck coinage claiming that they themselves were caliphs over the regions they ruled.

Attempts to rebuild the unity of the Muslim *umma* in the twentieth century have not worked. The shadowy and disputable caliphate of the Ottoman sultans was finally abolished in 1924 by Mustafa Kemal 'Atatürk' (1881–1938), 'the great Turk' for whom Turkish nationalism was more important than pan-Islamic unity. Upon independence in 1947, Pakistan was created from British India as a homeland for South Asian Muslims, in the name of religion. Yet in 1971, Bangladesh bloodily seceded from Pakistan; religion was a less important cement than racial, economic and political considerations.

Moreover, to assume the possibility and desirability of a united *umma* risks failing to recognize the pain of people who were dehumanized or dispossessed by the glory days of Islam. For example, in a recent BBC TV series *Living Islam* (published under that title by BBC Books in 1993), the Muslim scholar Akbar Ahmed laments the demise of Muslim Spain. He rightly praises its noble architecture, its intellectual achievements, and its tolerance towards minorities. Yet he records no sense of the Christian horror at the fall of Constantinople, nor does he show any empathetic recognition of the Christian anguish it caused. He recognizes that St Sophia was a marvel of architecture which has shaped the design of Muslim mosques since 1453, but that is all (Ahmed, *Living Islam*, 79). Yet mutual influence is surely of secondary importance to mutual understanding, which might have encouraged him to assess the religious significance of St Sophia and, indeed, Constantinople, for Eastern and other Christians. Nowadays, members of all religions should recognize and ponder upon the wounds their religion has caused others, rather than merely parading their own hurts and hopes.

Islamic attitudes towards other faiths have been shaped by its own political successes. Muslims expect to set the rules within which other communities operate, because very often they have been able do so. The decline of Muslim political power in the last three centuries has made most Muslims associate Islam's political impotence with their supposed religious disobedience. They then ask how it can be rectified, so that Muslims may again possess political power.

Some Muslims are beginning to ask whether relations need to be set on a different footing, one of mutual respect and tolerance. The contemporary meaning or even relevance of concepts like *jihad, jizya* and *ridda* are the subject of close and intense debate by Muslim scholars. One bold solution would be to consign them to the past, on the grounds that they are not appropriate today. They imply the necessity of a master–servant relationship of Islam towards other communities, instead of much-needed mutual respect and common justice. According to some Muslims, and non-Muslims, a great deal of past practice by Muslims has misread the *takbir*, the summons to the praise of God, *Allahu Akbar*, 'God is the greater', as *Islamu Akbar*, 'Islam is the greater'.

The life of the Prophet offers scope for the creation of a mindset different from the traditional Muslim one. When Muhammad died, he was master of most of Arabia, and Muslims were poised to spread Islam widely abroad. Yet for most of his career, the Prophet faced rejection and even persecution. Most Muslim commentators on Muhammad's political views and attitudes towards other communities stress his political and religious successes. When they mention his earlier struggles for support, or even failures to get it, they do so to make a contrast with his ultimate achievements. This is a perfectly proper thing to do. Another possibility, however, would be to explore his Makkan and early Madinan years for clues about how to live faithfully as a minority. At first blush, Muhammad's and the Quran's attitudes towards the pagan Quraysh, the Madinan Jews and Christians, and the *munafiqun* do not seem to point to a more constructive and tolerant attitude to alternative communities within a context of religious pluralism. But the simple fact is that Muhammad, for most of his ministry, presided over a minority community and exercised limited authority in the wider political and religious scene. This is surely worth pondering.

There is also another possibility, which is that the different interpretations of the household of Islam will learn from each other ways of living faithfully in the contemporary world. For centuries, Sunni and Shia Muslims have regarded each other with deep suspicion. Within the last decade, however, Shia Iran has become the focus for the hopes and support of many Sunni Muslims. One major reason is that the Iranian leaders have stood up against enemies of Islam, as Muslims see them. It was Iran which led the campaign against Salman Rushdie's controversial novel, *The Satanic Verses*, considered by most Muslims to be anti-Islamic. Iran has also focused Muslim discontent with Western cultural and economic domination, especially that of the USA.

Support for Shia leaders by Sunni Muslims is limited and may not last long. Ironically, it has been made possible by aspects of globalization against which many Muslim leaders are in open revolt. The existence of newspapers, telecommunications and the Internet make possible the widespread dissemination of information. New alliances can be forged, however temporary. How Muslims will operate such alliances, and what effect they may have upon Islam's sense of internal coherence and identity, and its relations to other communities, are intriguing uncertainties in the contemporary world.

Muhammad *and the* Role *of* Women

The place of women in human communities has been much discussed in the last two decades. The world's religions stand accused of being patriarchal and misogynistic by many of their own committed members, as well as by outsiders.

According to Muslims, Islam is, or should be, the ideal community. However, many generations of Western scholars of Islam have accused it of lowering the status of women. They point to the example of its Prophet, the theory of its teaching, and the practice of its men. They emphasize such things as the veiling of women; female seclusion; and the practice of female circumcision in large parts of the Muslim world. These accusations have naturally made many Muslims unwilling to examine Islam's record on women's rights and roles, or else excessively defensive or idealistic in their descriptions, lest biased detractors of their religion should distort the theory and practice of Islam's teaching about women.

This chapter looks at aspects of the teaching of the Quran and *Sharia* about the position of women. It explores issues surrounding the Prophet's polygamous marriages, then examines the importance of Aisha, the Prophet's favourite wife according to many Muslims. Finally, it asks what implications arise for the role of women in the contemporary Muslim world, and whether Muhammad's words and deeds can be interpreted to offer a new, more liberating vision for men and women, if that is what is required.

The Quran, the *Sharia* and Women

This section draws attention to the broad outlines of some of the views expressed there in the quranic revelation. Although there are no female prophets, some women are important positive figures in sacred history, mentioned in the Quran and elaborated in Islamic tradition. Three examples are: Eve; the wife of Pharaoh whose words of faith are recorded in Q66.11; and Mary, the mother of Jesus. On the other hand, the wickedness and terrible fate of the wives of Noah and Lot are 'examples to the unbelievers' (Q66.10). So, the position of women in the Quran, as also in the *Sharia*, is described in varied ways.

According to the Quran, the first human being was Adam. God then provided him with a wife, who is not named though the *hadith* call her Hawwa (in English, Eve). However, these facts do not endow men with innate superiority over women since the Quran insists that both come from a common origin:

> O humankind! Revere your sustainer who created you from a single person, and created from it its companion, and from both disseminated numerous men and women. (Q4.1)

The word here translated 'person' (in Arabic, *nafs*) is grammatically feminine. Some writers have made much of this, claiming that the first human being is feminine. For others, the use of *nafs* does not seem theologically or legally significant, else it would contradict quranic accounts of the creation of humankind; in their view, it is simply an accident of language. At any rate, the major point of the passage is that both men and women can obey God. The Quran says to humankind: 'I shall never waste the endeavour of any worker among you, whether male or female' (Q3.195). Equally, both Adam and his wife were together responsible for disobeying God. The Quran states that: 'Satan made them stumble from the garden, and so deprived them of their previous state' (Q2.36). Unlike the biblical account, the woman was not instrumental in tempting her mate into rebelliousness.

There are ritual ablutions prescribed in Muslim law which women must perform, the *ghusl*, 'greater ablution', for example, after childbirth and menstruation. Yet so must men after they have had an emission of semen, or for certain other prescribed reasons specific to their sex. The issues to do with purity in Islam signify neither the preeminence of men nor the wickedness of women, though some Muslims have misread the evidence to these ends. Islam stresses the need for both men and women to achieve inner and outer purity, and the Quran and *Sharia* provide means for both sexes to achieve that goal. The means to that end differ because men and women differ from one another in important ways.

Islam teaches the complementarity of the sexes. God's word reveals that all things from the beginning of creation were made in pairs (e.g. Q13.3, 51.49). There is, however, a distinctive, numinous quality about the relationship between men and women of the human species. The Quran says: 'O humankind! We have made you from a male and a female, and in nations and tribes so that you may know one another' (Q49.13). Knowledge is a multivalent quality denoting, among other things, sexual attraction and intuitive discernment. The mystery of relations between the sexes, hinted at in the Quran, is unfolded in the story of Adam's and Hawwa's expulsion from the garden. They were separated at that time, but met again at Arafat, a plain about thirteen miles from Makka. 'Arafat' comes from an Arabic verb meaning 'to recognize one another'. Human beings were not created to live alone, but find their deepest meaning in relations with one another.

Does complementarity favour men, or is this an enriching symbiotic relationship mutually advantageous to both sexes? Certain aspects of the marriage relationship sharply illustrate the respective roles of men and women. In Islam, marriages are not made in heaven but here on earth: they are not sacramental in quality, but matters for a legal contract between assenting adults. This does not make them inferior to Christian and other forms of marriage, as many non-Muslim polemicists assert. It is characteristic of Islam to deal with matters related to marriage as part of religious law, so that participants can know that they are following God's will laid down in it.

Legally, marriage in Islam has three requirements. It must be freely entered into by two adults. It is usually arranged by parents, though children have a right to reject such arrangements when they reach adulthood (often nine years of age for a girl, and twelve for a boy). The second requirement is that two male witnesses must be present at a marriage or, less usually, three people if only one witness is a man (see Q2.282, a passage which actually refers to contracting a debt or engaging in trade, and only by extension to witnessing a marriage). Finally, there are two dowries, both given to the bride by the groom.

The first consists of gifts of jewellery and clothing before the wedding takes place. These cannot be taken back without the bride's consent. The second is a commitment of financial support for the wife, in the event of the marriage failing. Both dowries ensure that a woman has her own financial and property rights, separate from her husband's.

The establishment of a woman's independent means balances the fact that divorce is much easier for a man than a woman. He can opt for repudiation of his spouse in front of witnesses, whereas she has the more exacting task of appealing to the decision of a religious court, where she has to establish a legal reason for the marriage to end, such as cruelty, adultery or (in some legal schools) her husband's failure to support her economically. The children of a marriage depend upon paternal acknowledgement in order to inherit from him. So, after a divorce, a woman is forbidden to remarry for three months. This determines whether she is pregnant by the man who is repudiating her.

This brief description of the arrangements for marriage and divorce illustrates a certain ambiguity about the comparative status of men and women in Islam. In marriage, women are accorded an honoured role, particularly that of mother: an oft-quoted *hadith* records that 'Paradise lies at the feet of the mother', indicating that she has the major responsibility for teaching her offspring, by word and deed, the basic teaching of Islam.

However, in the modern world, some Muslim women contend that the laws and customs which relate to marriage unfairly favour men, on the grounds that they are interpreted by men to further their own power over women. The liberal modernist Syed Ameer Ali asserted that 'women always have been and always will be, what men make them',[1] illustrating how easily even an enlightened man can reflect the prejudices of centuries. This raises issues of theory and practice: is the ideological structure of Islam inimical to women, or has it been abused by men in certain important instances?

To put this another way: do most men actually observe the divine commandments enshrined in the Quran and the *Sharia*, or do they manipulate them to their own advantage? Some women have been forced to pay the equivalent of a dowry, under the guise of a freewill gift, in order to contract what their fathers regard as a favourable marriage. Some, after a divorce, have been coerced into signing away their right to the second dowry. This means that the economic security of many women may be more apparent than real.

1. Ali, 'The Influence of Women in Islam', *The Nineteenth Century*, 45, May 1899, 756.

The clearest measure of a woman's autonomy is her economic independence from men. This can be measured not only by safeguards against divorce made for her in the marriage relationship, but also in her right to inherit from her father. The Quran establishes this prerogative:

> Regarding your children, God directs: to the male, a portion equal to that of two females; if there are only daughters, two or more, their share is two-thirds of the inheritance, but if only one, her share is a half. Parents receive a sixth share of the inheritance, if the deceased left children. If there are no children, and the parents are the heirs, then the mother has a third; but if the deceased left brothers, the mother has a sixth. This is after the payment of legacies and debts. You do not know whether your parents or your children are more useful to you. These are ordained by God; and God is All-knowing, All-wise . . . Your wife inherits a quarter of what you leave at death if you die childless, or else an eighth, after the payment of legacies and debts. (Q4.11f.)

Thus a woman inherits from her husband and children, but less than men. Many Muslims claim that this was a considerable improvement upon pre-Islamic arrangements. Muslims who justify quranic laws of inheritance and their development in the *Sharia* point to the fact that, under Islamic law, a woman's property is her own, to use as she will. Her father, husband and sons need more, since they are responsible for feeding, clothing and sheltering the family. Again, this may be more theoretically convincing than actually true. Much depends on local customs in different parts of the Muslim world. In many cases, women have no independent means, whatever the Quran and developed Muslim religious law might prescribe. Thus, it is a contentious issue whether Muslim laws of inheritance, in practice rather than theory, undergird women's rights.

Some Muslims go further than arguing about details and assert that, more than anyone else in history, Muhammad was responsible for improving the lot of women. For example, Syed Ameer Ali, writing in 1873, observed that

> Mohammed had proclaimed as one of the essential teachings of his creed, respect for women. Islam secured them rights, allowed them privileges, and put them on a footing of complete equality with men, excepting so far as physical differences went. (Ali, *A Critical Examination of the Life and Teachings of Mohammed*, 244)

Elsewhere, he noted that only during his own student years in England, with the passing of the Married Women's Property Act in 1873, did English law, built upon Christian foundations, permit wives the right to their own property and earnings, independent of their husband's control.[2] Yet this right had been enshrined in early Islam by the Prophet's teaching.

This claim that Muhammad's teaching immeasurably improved the lot of women needs careful nuancing, not mere assertion or the comparison of the theory of one religion with the practice of another. After all, Muhammad's first marriage was to a rich widow, who had prospered in the *jahiliyya*. Doubtless, many women had not done so, just as many flourish under Islamic law whereas others do not.

Sometimes, what men have made of women in Islam (as, of course, in other religions and in the secular world, too) has arguably demeaned both sexes. We have noted that marriage in Islam, though not sacramental, binds a man and a woman together in a complementary, mysterious, enriching relationship. Furthermore, it affords women economic security. Yet there are more controversial aspects of marriage in Islam.

Muta is a form of marriage permitted only by the majority branch of Shia Islam. It is contracted for a short duration, even of just one night. A fee and not a dowry is given. Most Muslims regard it as little better than licensed prostitution.

A more important matter is the permission Islam gives to men to practise polygamy. This certainly seems to illustrate the exploitation of women by men. Undoubtedly, polygamy (more properly polygyny, the marriage of one man to more than one woman) is permitted by the Quran:

> If you feel that you cannot deal with equity towards orphans, then marry women of your choice, two, three or four. But if you cannot act with equity towards them, then only one. (Q4.3)

Some Muslims have contended that since it is impossible to act even-handedly towards more than one woman in the institution of marriage, this verse is equivalent to a command to observe monogamy. Yet it is hard to see why the Quran should legislate for an impossibility. A more convincing clarification of the meaning of this verse takes into account its context in the early days of Islam. The battles between the Muslims

2.   Ali, 'Memoirs', *Islamic Culture*, 5, October 1931, 533.

and their Makkan opponents led to the creation of believing widows and orphans who needed the protection of marriage in order to find economic succour. Polygyny was one way, arguably temporary in intention, of providing such security. If so, then its practice by the Prophet and his earliest followers was not an exploitation of women's powerlessness, but a means of providing them with the stability of family life.

The Prophet himself had many more than four wives. In all, he married about ten times and also had one important concubine, Mariya the Copt, mother of his son, Ibrahim. Many Muslims regard Mariya as Muhammad's wife, a status conferred upon her by the birth of her son. What information does the Prophet's private life furnish about the role of women in Islam?

Muhammad's Marriages

Broadly speaking, there are two ways in which Muhammad's practice of polygamy has been interpreted by relatively recent scholars of Islam. The first, common among Muslim modernists, has been to defend his marriages as necessary acts of state or of compassion, irrelevant to his private needs. Indeed, in so far as we can discern his private physical and emotional needs, they were fulfilled for most of his adult life by one woman. Muhammad was twenty-five when he contracted his first marriage, to Khadija, a wealthy widow some fifteen years older than him. During her lifetime, he took no other wife. One reason for this must have been the close relationship they shared. She comforted and supported him in the early years of his ministry in Makka. Her death was a blow to him, not only because of her economic support, but also (as we shall see below, in discussing Khadija's and Aisha's status as wives of the Prophet) for more intimate reasons.

After Khadija's death, Muhammad's other marriages were conducted for the public good: he had to protect vulnerable widows and orphans, or else conclude important compacts with friends and foes. He was about fifty when he married a second time, to Sauda, a widow who was herself over forty years old. She had been an emigrant to Abyssinia, and deserved the Prophet's protection. Moreover, she could be a stepmother to his motherless children. His third wife, Aisha, was the daughter of Abu Bakr, one of his staunchest and earliest supporters. Muhammad's fourth wife was Hafsa, the daughter of

Umar, who would become the second caliph. She was the widow of a man who was killed in the Battle of Badr, and this marriage was therefore both an act of compassion and also an alliance with an important man. In similar fashion, other marriages of Muhammad can be explained on compassionate or political grounds. None was for carnal pleasure.

A second view, common until relatively recently among Western Christian scholars, is that, freed from the restraining dominant influence of Khadija, Muhammad in his later years was free to indulge sensual appetites which he had hitherto suppressed. A notable nineteenth-century Christian biographer of Muhammad, Sir William Muir (1819–1905), an important government official in British India, wrote that

> In his youth he [Muhammad] lived a virtuous life . . . Yet it is remarkable that during this period were composed most of those passages of the Koran in which the black-eyed 'Houries' [more properly *huriyya*, virginal females], reserved for Believers in Paradise, are depicted in such glowing colours . . . [It] was not until the mature age of fifty-four that he made the dangerous trial of polygamy, by taking Aisha, yet a child, as the rival of Sauda. Once the natural limits of restraint were overpassed, Mohammed fell a prey to his strong passion for the sex . . . [His] desires were not to be satisfied by the range of a harim already in advance of Arab custom, and more numerous than was permitted to any of his followers; rather, as age advanced they were stimulated to seek for a new and varied indulgence. A few months after his nuptials with Zeinab and Um Selama, the charms of a second Zeinab were by accident discovered too fully before his admiring gaze. She was the wife of Zeid, his adopted son and bosom friend; but he was unable to smother the flame she had kindled in his breast; and, by divine command, she was taken to his embrace. (Muir, *The Life of Mohammed*, revised T. H. Weir, 514f.)

Muhammad's marriage to Zaynab bint Jahsh illustrates the gulf between Muslim modernists and many Western Christian scholars. She was a young widow when she emigrated to Madina, and married Zayd bin Haritha at Muhammad's instigation. Disapproving Western scholars argue that in marrying her, Muhammad overstepped the boundaries of seemliness and good taste: she was as a daughter to him, yet he nevertheless connived at her divorce so that he could gratify his lust for her. Such writers rely largely on the account given by the Muslim historian, Tabari, who recorded that Muhammad was so struck by Zaynab's beauty when he accidentally came upon her alone and in loose and scanty dress, that he exclaimed, 'Gracious Lord! Good heavens! How you do turn over the hearts of men!' Zaynab, overhearing him, was flattered by these words and boasted of them to her husband. Zayd went to Muhammad and offered to divorce her. Muhammad resisted his proposal, but Zayd went ahead and repudiated her. Still Muhammad hesitated, but finally married her after receiving divine approval to do so.

Muslim modernists defend the Prophet against the charge that he was sexually attracted to Zaynab. They point out that she was Muhammad's cousin, known to him since childhood. She was also thirty-eight (or thirty-five) years old, and therefore past the bloom of youthful beauty. She was unhappy in her marriage to Zayd, thinking him her social inferior. Muhammad married her because he felt responsible for her, since he had arranged her unhappy marriage to Zayd.

In this instance, Muslim modernists seem to be unconvincingly defensive. Elements of their justification are not persuasive. For example: why should a revered Muslim historian record this story, if it were not true? Would Muhammad have married a social snob, when his divine community was based on other, more impressive, foundations? Why should older women not be sexually attractive to a middle-aged man? (Indeed, Zaynab was, though a mature woman, still much younger than Muhammad.)

Certainly, the Quran justifies the marriage in a passage which strikes a defensive note, as though God had to protect Muhammad from public disapproval and his own inner misgivings:

> You said to one who had received God's favour and yours: 'Retain your wife, and fear God', while you hid in your heart that which God was about to reveal. You feared the people, but it is more fitting that you should fear God. Then when Zayd had fulfilled his purpose with her, we joined her in marriage to you so that there may be no difficulty to the believers in marrying wives of their adopted sons, when the latter have accomplished what must be done with them. God's command must be fulfilled! The Prophet is not to be criticized for what God has determined he must do. (Q33.37f.)

This passage claims that the Prophet does not need to justify his actions to people, but must only obey God. Nevertheless, it offers one vindication of Muhammad's marriage to Zaynab, in that it abolishes the prohibition against marrying the wives of adopted sons. This custom had previously been forbidden, and the condemnation of the Prophet which the quranic passage reflects would have arisen from his breaking this social taboo. After this passage was revealed, public criticism of Muhammad by his followers died away.

Neither the Muslim modernist nor Western Christian interpretations of Muhammad's marriages are entirely convincing. Many people's view of sexual prowess has always been far removed from modernist Muslims' apologetic concerns and from Muir's Victorian scruples. One *hadith*, recorded by Ibn Sad (d. 845), affirms that Muhammad was able to satisfy sexually all his wives each night. No doubt this overstates the case, but it displays that frank enjoyment of sex which Islamic law encourages all men and women to find within marriage.

The picture of the Prophet which emerges is of a man who made many of his marriages for reasons of state or to cement an alliance, but who was not free from the occasional pangs of violent physical attraction, any more than are most other men and women. An intriguing fact is that, with the exception of Mariya and one other concubine, he seems to have married all the women he sexually desired.

Muhammad was thus a man for whom the institution of marriage was a central concern. Yet the form of marriage instituted by Islam was far removed from the modern Western idealization of the nuclear family (a model which itself is increasingly under question and threat even in the West). Polygamy was practised in sixth- and seventh-century Arabia (though how common it was is a matter of debate), and people lived in extended families.

The Prophet's family was a special case, precisely because of his vocation. At the time of his marriage to Zaynab bint Jahsh, Muhammad placed restrictions on the freedom of his wives. The *hijab* verse, according to most *hadith*, was revealed because some guests lingered overlong at the wedding feast in Zaynab's house:

> Believers! Do not enter the Prophet's houses for a meal before its preparation until leave is given you; enter when you are invited and leave when you have taken your meal without engaging in familiar talk. This annoys the Prophet, who is ashamed to dismiss you, though God is not ashamed of the truth. And when you ask his wives for anything you want, ask them from behind a veil [*hijab*], which is for greater purity for

your hearts and for theirs. Neither is it right that you should annoy God's Apostle, or that you should ever marry his widows after him. Truly this would be a grave matter in God's sight. (Q33.53)

Until the occasion of this verse, Muhammad's wives had taken a full part in the life of Madina. Thereafter they could not. Soon after this occasion, another revelation enjoined Muhammad's wives and all other believing women to cover themselves in cloaks when abroad 'so that they may be recognized and not molested' by the hypocrites, and those whose hearts were diseased, and those who fomented strife in the city (Q33.59f.).

The custom of *purda* was instituted shortly afterwards. Yet its more rigorous practice, where women are swathed from head to foot and secluded from most men, is not commended by the Quran, which mentions only the need for women to pursue modesty (which is also enjoined upon men in the previous verse):

And say to the believing women that they should lower their gaze and guard their chastity, and that they should not display their charms more than ordinarily appears. They should draw their veils over their bosoms and not display their charms except to their husbands, their fathers, their fathers-in-law, their sons or step-sons, their brothers or their brothers' sons, or their sisters' sons, or their women, or anyone whom their right hands possess, or male servants free of physical desires, or small children who have no awareness of sex. They should not stamp their feet in order to draw attention to their hidden ornaments. Believers! Turn, all of you, towards God, that you may prosper. (Q24.31)

At some point in the Madinan years, the divine word commanded Muhammad's wives to choose between 'God and his Prophet' and 'the world and its adornment' (Q33.28f.). This revelation came at the end of a month when, to punish them, the Prophet had kept aloof from all of his wives. The *hadith* offer various reasons for what led to this period of separation. Some say that the wives were jealous of the Prophet's relations with Mariya the Copt. Others link it to an occasion when two of the wives conspired against him, and he threatened to divorce them (Q66.4f.). At any rate, this 'verse of choice' led his wives to choose God and him, not the world and its adornment.

Muhammad's wives were certainly distinguished from other women by what was required of them. A cluster of quranic verses, Q33.30–4, generally believed to have been revealed soon after the 'verse of choice', enjoin precise and sweeping constraints upon their freedom of movement and deportment:

> Wives of the Prophet, whoever among you commits an evidently shameful act will receive a double punishment: this is how God inevitably operates. But whoever among you obeys God and his Prophet and does right will be given a double reward by us, and we have a rich preparation for her. Wives of the Prophet, you are not like other women. If you remember God, do not be too open in your speech, lest a person with a diseased heart should covet you; so say only conventional words. Stay at home, and do not deck yourself out showily as in the days of ignorance. Say your prayers and give alms, and obey God and his Prophet. God wants to remove any filth from you, people of this house, and to cleanse you thoroughly. Remember any of God's signs and wisdom recited in your homes. God is observant and informed.

According to one common tradition, Muhammad said that the merit earned by men fighting for the cause of God is like that gained by women who stay quietly at home and who cannot therefore be used by Satan to corrupt society. If true, then Muhammad probably interpreted the restrictions imposed on his wives as exemplary for all Muslim women. Certainly, these constraints enshrine domesticity as a virtue: the home becomes the sacred space for women to fulfil their godly function of honouring their husbands and bringing up children. Eventually, the Prophet's wives were reverenced as 'mothers of the believers', whom Muslims might not marry after his death (Q33.6, 53).

Aisha

Along with the Prophet's daughter Fatima, his first wife Khadija, and a few other quranic figures such as Mary, the mother of Jesus, Aisha is held in special affection and esteem throughout the Sunni Muslim world. Many Muslims believe that her superiority to other wives of the Prophet except Khadija lies in certain endowments no others shared. These include: she was a virgin when she married the Prophet; both of her parents were emigrants to Madina; she saw Gabriel, who had brought her likeness to Muhammad; Muhammad received revelation in her presence; Muhammad was buried under her living quarters.

Aisha was betrothed to the Prophet by her father, Abu Bakr, when she was six or seven years old. She is said to have remembered the consummation of her marriage. She described how she was playing with her friends on a swing when her mother called her and took her to a house. Muhammad had sex with her when the guests left. She was nine years old, and her husband about fifty-three. Modern readers might find this story poignant or even repugnant, though neither Aisha nor other contemporaries found it so. Muhammad certainly enjoyed her company for more than its sexual gratification, acting tenderly towards her and playing with her and her toys.

Although Aisha was a young woman, or perhaps because she was, with all the confidence and naivety of youth, she was not afraid to speak her mind to her husband or even implicitly to criticize her husband to others. When some Madinans spread the rumour that Muhammad kept some of God's revelation to himself and did not share it with others, Aisha made a scathing comment about the quranic verses which justified her husband's marriage to Zaynab. She said that 'If the Prophet had concealed anything of the revelation, it would have been those verses he ought to have kept hidden.' Her remark to her husband about Q33.50, which revealed the range of women whom the Prophet was permitted to marry, was even sharper: 'God is in a hurry to satisfy your desires.' Aisha was surely not expressing the cynicism of those for whom the revelation seems a mere convenience. Rather, her words betray the bitterness of a young woman who did not want more rivals for her husband's affection, which bestowed on her the little authority she possessed.

Certainly, she was not in awe of Muhammad and showed considerable bravery during the accusations of adultery that were whispered about her when she was no more than fourteen years old, perhaps even a year or two younger. She had gone with Muhammad on a military expedition. Early one morning, on the way back to Madina, she went to answer a call of nature. She delayed returning to the camp because she realized she had lost her necklace and lingered to find it. When she got back, everyone had left, thinking that she was in her litter which had been placed on the back of a camel. Sensibly, she did not panic, and stayed in the deserted camp. Eventually and by chance, a young man passed by with a camel, on which he and Aisha returned to Madina. Gossip spread like a fire, initiated by Muhammad's bitter opponent, Abdallah ibn Ubayy. Interestingly, a sister of Zaynab bint Jahsh is also named as another of the instigators, which may indicate that there was considerable jostling for influence and prestige among Muhammad's wives (or that Zaynab sought revenge for Aisha's jibe about the revelation which permitted her – Zaynab's – marriage to the Prophet). Aisha was ill with a fever when she returned to Madina, and only guessed that she was in trouble because Muhammad was uncharacteristically cool towards her.

The Prophet was in a quandary. He questioned two people as character witnesses. One recommended that Aisha be considered innocent. The other, Ali, was less supportive. He told Muhammad that 'women are plentiful, and you can easily exchange one for another', and is said to have tried to beat the truth out of Aisha's slave girl. Even Aisha's parents were sceptical of her blamelessness. Perhaps their coolness towards her arose from more than a pious and overriding desire to obey God and his Prophet: they were placing a distance between themselves and their daughter so that they and their family interests would survive if she did not. Be that as it may, Aisha stood up to them and to her husband's doubts. She refused to apologize for a wrong she had not committed and, despite weeping many tears, stoutly maintained that she would bear her ordeal patiently like one of the patriarchs. A month later, the revelation of Q24.11–26 established Aisha's innocence. It also criticized Muslims who had gossiped about her, and established harsh penalties in the future life against all who slandered chaste women. Further laws against slandering chaste women are found in Q24.4, where an accuser is condemned to eighty lashes unless he brings four witnesses.

Pious recorders of traditions make much of Aisha's trust in God to vindicate her. In this they are joined by more sceptical Western biographers of the Prophet: according to Muir, she 'resumed her place, more secure than ever, as the queen of the Prophet's heart and home' (Muir, *The Life of Mohammed*, 304). Muhammad never ceased to love her, which is touchingly illustrated by the fact that, against his custom of staying each night with a different wife, his last days were spent in Aisha's apartments and he died in her arms. Yet, even so, during the time slander swirled around her she must have been terrified at the possibility of being judged guilty by her husband. Her social standing, even her life and death, lay in his hands.

Aisha probably never forgot Ali's role in her humiliation. In 656, she led the Battle of the Camel against him. The reasons given for this are several and varied. One might have been revenge, long nurtured and at last given opportunity to be vented. Another more important motive was her involvement in the struggle for power among clans of the Quraysh in the years following the Prophet's death. As a daughter of Abu Bakr, who was chosen to replace Muhammad as political leader of the community when Ali expected to succeed, she represented other interests than Ali's, which might explain their mutual hostility. More speculatively, perhaps her involvement in the civil war against Ali was an attempt to free herself from the restrictions that were placed upon the widows of the Prophet. After all, she was only about eighteen years old when Muhammad died. However much she loved him, the honoured but confined role she was expected to follow, though edifying to many Muslim men and women then and since, might have seemed impossibly stifling to the spirited young women she appears to have been. Her revolt failed and Ali confined her to the role prescribed by quranic injunction. She died in Madina in 678, aged about sixty-four years old.

In the last two decades of her life, she communicated her detailed eye-witness observations of her husband's words and actions to male and female believers. Thus, in Sunni Islam she is venerated as an important source of *hadith*, many of which contributed to the establishment of the *Sharia*.

She has become particularly important to many modern Muslim feminists for debunking many of the misogynistic traditions and their transmitters. For example, she noted of Abu Hurayra (d. *c.*678), who is said to have narrated an immense number of *hadith*, including many disdainful of women, that 'He is not a good listener, and when he is asked a question he gives wrong answers.' On one occasion, she refuted one of his *hadith* which ran: 'Three things bring bad luck: house, woman, and horse.' Aisha explained that

> He came into our house when the Prophet was in the middle of a sentence. He only heard the end of it. What the Prophet said was: 'May Allah refute the Jews; they say three things bring bad luck: house, woman, and horse.' (Mernissi, *Women and Islam*, 76)

Not surprisingly, Aisha and Abu Hurayra did not get on, as this account illustrates:

> When she said to him, 'Abu Hurayra, you relate Hadith that you never heard,' he replied sharply, 'O Mother, all I did was collect Hadith, while you were too busy with kohl [a kind of eye-shadow] and your mirror.' (Ibid., 72)

Although Abu Hurayra is remembered as a pious man, and the most revered collections of the *hadith* incorporate some of his material,

Aisha may have had a point. The caliph Umar, a notable misogynist, is supposed to have said, in relation to remembering *hadith*: 'We have many things to say, but we are afraid to say them, and that man there [Abu Hurayra] has no restraint' (ibid., 79).

Shia Muslims do not see Aisha as an exemplary figure. Her enmity with Ali, and her father's usurpation (as Shias see it) of Ali's rightful role as successor of the Prophet, lead them to play down her importance as a positive role model in the history of Islam. Many depict her as a scheming, ambitious woman. The quranic verses which Sunni Muslims interpret as exonerating Aisha from the charge of adultery do not actually mention her by name. Later Shia commentators reject her innocence and believe that the verses have a different focus. Some argue that they do not refer to Aisha as the object of slander but as one who spread, or was even the source of, defamation against Mariya the Copt.

Syed Ameer Ali, a Shia Muslim as well as an apologist for Islam against Western calumnies, reveals in subtle but clear ways his community's verdict upon Aisha. In his judgement, Muhammad chose Aisha's house to stay in during his final illness because it was 'close to the mosque'; he does not mention that Muhammad loved her above all his wives and died in her arms. He also maintained that her involvement in the Battle of the Camel was partly because 'this lady had always borne an inveterate dislike towards the son-in-law of Khadija, and now this feeling had grown into positive hatred' (Ali, *The Spirit of Islam*, 117, 296). This was a clever way of indicating her jealousy towards Muhammad's first wife, a common supposition among Shia Muslims.

Actually, there is some reason to believe that Aisha was resentful of her illustrious predecessor. She is recorded as saying, 'I was not jealous of any of the wives of the Prophet except Khadija, even though I came [after] her death.' She earned a rare rebuke from the Prophet when she referred to Khadija as that 'toothless old woman whom God has replaced with a better'. The Prophet corrected her:

Not so. God has not replaced her with a better. She believed in me when I was rejected. When they called me a liar, she declared I was truthful. When I was poor, she shared her wealth with me; and God granted her children, withholding them from other women. (Spellberg, *Politics, Gender, and the Islamic Past: The Legacy of 'A'isha bint Abi Bakr*, 155)

Khadija and Aisha make a fascinating comparison. Khadija's formative years and most of her life was spent in the *jahiliyya*. She was in her middle fifties when Muhammad received his first revelation, and died less than ten years later. Hers was a successful life. She was a wealthy widow, a merchant, for whom the Prophet worked before their marriage. Her economic support of him, and her emotional comfort during the early difficult years of his ministry suggest that she was a strong, perhaps even domineering woman. Whatever pious condemnations Muslims make about pre-Islamic Arabian ignorance, and however it affected for evil many women, she had prospered.

In contrast, Aisha spent all her life under Islam. She was born about 614, after her father had embraced Islam. She too was a determined, even plucky, woman of considerable character. Her caustic wit and awareness of her own importance shine through many of the *hadith* attributed to her, and the accounts related of her. Yet her life under the early years of Islam was much more circumscribed than Khadija's had been. Her marriage was lived out under the public gaze, and gradually she and the other wives were compelled to live a secluded existence, even though given immense deference and respect. Widowed at about eighteen years old, she lived her remaining almost fifty years in honour, but under the restrictions imposed by the quranic revelation on all Muhammad's wives. When she died, any hope that she might be buried alongside her husband died with her. He is buried in her quarters, next to her father, Abu Bakr, and the second caliph, Umar. Many Muslims believe that there is a place for Jesus, when he comes again to set in motion the end of the world and must die. But there is no room for the Prophet's favourite wife to lie next to her husband in her own apartments.

Of course, most Muslims regard Aisha's life as privileged and fulfilled: a rare honour indeed, in their estimation, to be the much loved wife of the seal of the prophets. Maybe she, too, thought of her life as a success story. However, there were other lives she could have lived. She might have been the Prophet's wife under what some women (and men) might interpret as a more liberating dispensation of heaven; or else an unknown but happy wife to someone else, and mother of his children. Although Ameer Ali was not an admirer of Aisha's, his comment about women could refer poignantly to her. She was indeed what men made her.

Variant Sunni and Shia convictions about her, and her importance to contemporary Muslim feminists, suggest that she has long been interpreted by other Muslims, until recently almost entirely by men, to justify their reading of sacred history. Despite her feisty character and important role in transmitting accounts of the Prophet's words and deeds, it is difficult, some would say impossible, to separate her own concerns, ideals and hopes from the interpretations others, almost always men, have laid upon her.

Muslim Women *in the* Contemporary World

This examination of Muhammad and the role of women in Islam raises three serious issues for contemporary Muslims and others: how far, if at all, is the Prophet's attitude to women a pattern for all believers? What is the relationship between the Quran and Muhammad? Does it matter that Islamic theory about women diverges from the practice of Muslim men?

We have seen in chapter 2 that Muhammad's life and teaching are exemplary for Muslims, who pattern their lives on his words and deeds. Nevertheless, Muslims carefully distinguish between God's words and his own. Sometimes, indeed, Muhammad admitted that his own opinion yielded poor advice. So it would be possible for Muslims to argue that Muhammad was mistaken in some of his attitudes towards women, though this has rarely been done.

More common have been attempts to interpret the Prophet's practice in the light of the times and place in which he lived. Muslim modernists like Syed Ameer Ali have done this in broad brush-strokes:

> With the progress of thought, with the ever-changing conditions of this world, the necessity for polygamy disappears, and its practice is tacitly abandoned or expressly forbidden. And hence it is, that in those Moslem countries where the circumstances which made its existence at first necessary are disappearing, plurality of wives has come to be regarded as an evil, and as an institution opposed to the teachings of the Prophet; while in those countries where the conditions of society are different, where the means which, in advanced communities, enable women to help themselves are absent or wanting, polygamy must necessarily continue to exist. (Ali, *The Spirit of Islam*, 230)

Ameer Ali's argument is that Muhammad's situation is very different from the modern world's and prescriptions for it need not any longer bind all Muslim women. Certainly, most Muslims believe that certain quranic verses had their force abrogated during the lifetime of the Prophet, because new situations called forth new duties. Moreover, the collections of *hadith* pay close attention to the importance of the date and context of quranic revelations and prophetic words and deeds, and do not simply commend them as acontextual rules for sound belief and behaviour. Nevertheless, many Muslims act as though the Prophet were a supra-historical person whose words and deeds can easily be applied to any time and place (just as, for example, some Christians treat Jesus in a like fashion). The question remains: can they? If not, then such Muslims need to amplify how the Prophet's life remains exemplary for Muslims and, indeed, all who would strive to obey God's word in the contemporary world.

A more subtle way of emphasising the contextual importance of Prophetic action and quranic revelation is that of the Moroccan sociologist and feminist, Fatima Mernissi. For example, she claims that the *hijab* verse, commanding the Prophet's wives to speak to men from behind a veil, came for these women's protection. She depicts the Prophet as reluctantly forced by the misogynistic Umar to compromise his principles for the pragmatic value of providing security for his wives in the volatile aftermath of the siege of Madina by the Quraysh.[3] That expediency should have been temporary. What really matters is that Muhammad, unlike many contemporary Muslims

> acknowledged the importance of affection and sex in life. And, during expeditions, his wives were not just background figures, but shared with him his strategic concerns. (Mernissi, *The Veil and the Male Elite*, 104)

The implication is clear: Muslim men should follow the intention of Muhammad to engage with women as honoured companions. Mernissi and other Muslim feminists perform a valuable though controversial service in reminding their co-religionists that the quranic and *hadith* texts may have different and more limited implications than are found in the pious assumptions and acts of many Muslim men.

Conservative Muslims argue that such judgements are misguided and often malevolent. They tend to believe that many contemporary

3. Mernissi, *The Veil and the Male Elite*, 85ff., 162ff.

feminist expectations, whether of Muslims or other women, are contrary to the word of God, and their implementation must be resisted. Many Muslim feminists recognize that Western women's issues are not necessarily those appropriate to Muslim women, who must find their own path to a liberating future. What that path is, seems less clear. Understandably, many Muslim women are keen to avoid antagonizing conservative Muslim opinion so their private beliefs do not always gain a public airing.

If that path is to be followed it will need to challenge the unholy prevarications of some supposedly devout Muslim men. For example, the reformist South Asian Muslim political movement, the Jamaat-I-Islami, supported the unsuccessful candidacy of Fatima Jinnah in the Pakistani presidential elections of 1956. Ms Jinnah was the sister of Muhammad Ali Jinnah (d. 1948), who had led Pakistan to independence from British rule. Yet in recent years the Jamaat has claimed that Benazir Bhutto ought not to be Pakistan's Prime Minister, on the grounds that a woman cannot be the head of government. In both cases the Jamaat, though self-confessedly a party which seeks the conformity of Pakistan to Islamic laws, subordinated religious beliefs to what it vainly hoped would be political advantage. In doing so, it implied that a careful, coherent, creative Islamic understanding of the role of women was much less important than its own survival and triumphalism.

The route towards a more just role for women will also have to do more than condemn certain practices as un-Islamic. A custom like that of female circumcision is not commended in the teachings of the Prophet and Muslim law. It reflects centuries of cultural practice which usually pre-dates the coming of Islam to those areas. But by itself, this is not a convincing explanation of that custom's continuing hold in parts of the Muslim world. If Islam is meant to create a single community obedient to the one God, then it needs to ensure that the actions of those who follow it conform in large measure to its theory. Otherwise, what is its point?

Many Muslims, men and women, agree that the treatment of women by Muslim men is opposed to quranic injunction and the provisions of Islamic law. Yet this is often an easy judgement to make, a toothless and theoretical liberalism, unless it is backed by serious attempts to rectify grave injustices. Mernissi and others attempt to improve the lot of women by contrasting the prophet's attitude towards women with that of many Muslim men, even his contemporaries like Umar. The writings of Muslim feminists make for exciting yet equivocal reading. Which Muhammad are we and they to affirm? The polygamist patriarch or the devoted and consultative companion? Or are both possible and, if so, how? This leads us to the further questions, not least: who is Muhammad for today's world, and how may we find him?

Muhammad *in* Recent Debate

This chapter examines the various pictures of Muhammad which emerge from recent scholarship on the history of Islam. In doing so, it explores the meaning of Muhammad for both Muslims and non-Muslims.

Muhammad *and* Radical Western Scholars

This book has, by and large, accepted the corpus of Quran and *hadith*, and the works of other early Muslims, as reliable bases for describing the life, teachings and meaning of Muhammad. This is the witness of almost every Muslim, certainly of every Muslim who has been unhesitatingly accepted as such by the community of Islam. God's authorship of the Quran and its integrity as a work contained within Muhammad's ministry has been doubted by very few Muslims indeed (as we shall discuss below). The few Muslims who have suspected the historicity of much of the *hadith* literature, such as the Indian Muslim modernist, Sir Sayyid Ahmad Khan (1817–98), have been deeply controversial figures. Even an author like Fatima Mernissi, who questions the worth of many *hadith* about women found in the revered works of Bukhari and Muslim, does not doubt the truth of the *hadith* literature as a whole.

Non-Muslim scholars of Islam may have been more cautious in their approach, and have interpreted stories about the Prophet's words and exploits rather differently from pious Muslims. But they too have tended until recently to accept the early *maghazi* accounts of Muhammad's 'raiding campaigns' and the early *sira*, 'lives' or biographies of the Prophet, as material for constructing a chronological account of the quranic revelations.

Yet this consensus has begun to break down. The studies of Ignaz Goldziher and Joseph Schacht seriously questioned the authenticity of the *hadith* as a source for Muhammad's life.[1] Goldziher believed that they reveal the rich diversity of the Islamic community's development in its first two or three hundred years. Schacht contended that

> every legal tradition from the Prophet, until the contrary is proved, must be taken not as an authentic or essentially authentic, even if slightly obscured, statement valid for his time or the time of the Companions, but as the fictitious expression of a legal document formulated at a later date. (Schacht, *The Origins of Muhammadan Jurisprudence*, 149).

Until recently, most Western scholars of Islam, although they recognized the insights of Goldziher and Schacht, drew back from following their insights to radical conclusions. However, the last twenty years have seen the rise of radical Western scholars who not only doubt the historical value of the *hadith*, but have not hesitated to attack even the authenticity and integrity of the Quran.

In 1977, Patricia Crone and Michael Cook argued in their book, *Hagarism*, that although 'it is not unreasonable . . . [to present] a sensibly edited version of the tradition as historical fact', scholars could follow an alternative path.[2]

In their view the *maghazi-sira* works should be treated as sources for religious ideas current in the eighth century, when they circulated, not for a life of Muhammad. Crone and Cook looked outside the Muslim tradition for neglected non-Islamic sources, in order to piece together a fascinatingly novel account of the origins of Islam in which

---

1. Goldziher, *Muslim Studies*, 2 vols; Schacht, *The Origins of Muhammadan Jurisprudence*, 1971.
2. Crone and Cook, *Hagarism*, 3.

Muhammad, a merchant who became a preacher of monotheism to the Arabs, taught them that they were heirs, as descendants of Abraham, to the Promised Land. They were called the *muhajirun* by Crone and Cook because of the Arabs' belief that they were descended from Abraham through Hagar, as well as the importance they attached to the *hijra*. Crone and Cook drew here on a wider understanding of *muhajirun* than a specific reference to those 'emigrants' who went from Makka to Madina with Muhammad. In Muhammad's lifetime, the word was sometimes used to describe other individuals and groups who joined him thereafter. (Even today, it has been analogously employed to describe Pakistanis of Indian descent who emigrated to Pakistan after the partition of 1947.) Crone and Cook were probably right to detect a reference to Hagar in the word *muhajirun*: she was the mother of Abraham's son Ishmael, who came to be regarded as the ancestor of the Arabs.

According to Crone and Cook, the Arabs joined forces with Jews, exiled by the Persians, to recapture the Holy Land. Muhammad was still alive when Jerusalem was captured by Umar. Shortly afterwards, the Arabs broke with the Jews. Crone and Cook develop this interpretation with great verve and subtlety.

According to John Wansbrough the historical sources for early Islam are best described as 'Salvation History'.[3] They are theological justifications of Muhammad's importance, reflecting several viewpoints and created by many different interest groups. Their nature forbids us from knowing what actually happened in the days of Muhammad, still less in what order.

However, somewhat ironically, the hypotheses of Wansbrough, Cook, Crone and other radical historians often seem much more tenuously related to historical reality than the received opinions they criticize. Certainly, many of the non-Islamic sources referred to in *Hagarism* provide slender, insubstantial evidence for such a profound reinterpretation of Islamic origins and the life of Muhammad.

It is not just Muslim scholars who feel the weight of criticism by this radical scholarship. An older generation of Western scholars is also found wanting. Julian Baldick implicitly condemns William Montgomery Watt (b.1909) and Maxime Rodinson (b.1915) for their economic analysis of Makka (and in Rodinson's case, also his psychological portrait of Muhammad):

3. Wansbrough, *The Sectarian Milieu: Content and Composition of Islamic Salvation History.*

As for 'modern' portraits of Muhammad, in which Marxist sociological surveys rest on the flimsiest tatters of historical 'fact', and Freudian psychoanalysis is brought to bear on a personality who remains a shadow, the less said the better. (Clarke (ed.), 'Early Islam' in *The World's Religions: Islam*, 9)

There is some force in Baldick's argument. In particular, Watt's Marxist account of the origins of Islam (which was accepted by Rodinson, himself a Marxist) has been exploded in another book by Patricia Crone. Her *Meccan Trade and the Rise of Islam* dismisses Watt's thesis 'that a city in a remote corner of Arabia had some social problems to which a preacher responded by founding a world religion. It sounds like an overreaction' (235). Crone's evidence, marshalled in her book, that Mecca was not a town on important trading routes seems irrefutable. Less convincing is her alternative hypothesis, first outlined in *Hagarism*, that Islam originated elsewhere in north-west Arabia as an attempt to mobilize Arab identity and values against foreign, Persian domination (247).

Undoubtedly, some of the radical scholars' criticisms of more cautious non-Muslim scholars are potent. Watt, Rodinson and many occidental scholars of Islam accept the reliability of the sources believed by faithful Muslims more on confessional than on historical grounds. They run the risk of meriting Baldick's objection that 'to admit, as many do, that the sources are entirely unreliable, and then to construct a narrative based on them, is indefensible in logic' (Baldick, 'Early Islam', 10).

Some radical scholars insist that they are doing no more than applying to Islam tools that have long been used about other religions. Julian Baldick writes that

The standard Muslim biography of Muhammad, composed well over a hundred years after his death, and edited in the ninth century [Ibn Hisham's (d. 833 or 828) revision of Ibn Ishaq's (d. *c.*767) work], is the earliest extended narrative that we possess. Today no serious student of early Christianity would imagine that its beginnings could be reconstructed, or the life of Jesus convincingly retold, if so lengthy an interval existed between our sources and the period to which they refer. (Ibid., 9)

The radical scholars' insights pose serious problems for writing a biography of Muhammad. The safest judgement is that the study of the origins of Islam is at present in flux. There is no agreed methodology, and no assured results. It is an exciting time to assess the meaning of Muhammad, unless one is a conservative Muslim for whom the process is at best *bida*, godless innovation.

My own hunch is that the *maghazi-sira* works, the Quran itself and some of the *hadith* are challenged but not overturned as adequate bases for the task of painting a reasonably trustworthy portrait of the historical Muhammad. Even so, Western perceptions of the Prophet may look very different in twenty years' time. How far Muslims will acknowledge and profit from this process is open to question.

Muhammad *and the* Orientalists

Baldick's view that Muhammad is 'a personality who remains a shadow' contradicts the deepest Muslim convictions that his life is so open to the clear light of historical day that a follower's deeds and words can and must be based on them. Many Muslims interpret this radical position as the latest attempt to denigrate the Arabian Prophet and his religion by biased Westerners. Such critics and their predecessors have been summarily dismissed as 'Orientalists'.

The *Oxford English Dictionary* records that the first use of the word 'Orientalist' was in about 1780. It meant a student of the Orient. The designation 'Orientalism', the study of the East, dates back to 1812. In more recent decades, particularly during the last twenty years, 'Orientalism' and its other grammatical forms have been used in an unfavourable sense, mainly of Western scholars of Islam. They stand condemned of writing condescendingly about the Orient, and of being involved as agents of imperialism to bring about its denigration and devise the destruction of many of its religions and cultures. So, for example, Abdallah Laroui defined 'Orientalist' as 'a foreigner – in this case a westerner – who takes Islam as the subject of his research', and continued:

> we find in the Orientalists' work an ideological (in the crudest sense of the word) critique of Islamic culture. The result of great intellectual effort is for the most part valueless . . . The caste of Orientalists constitutes part of the bureaucracy and, for this reason, suffers from limitations that badly inhibit the free creation of new approaches or even the application of those that already exist. (Quoted in Watt, *Muslim–Christian Encounters*, 107)

The most scathing critique of Orientalism in recent years has been that of Edward Said (b. 1935), by origin a Palestinian Christian, now an American citizen and a secularist. In his influential book *Orientalism* (first published in 1978), he described and condemned the phenomenon in three long chapters: 'The Scope of Orientalism'; 'Orientalist Structures and Restructures'; and 'Orientalism Now'. Said's basic point, passionately made, is that 'modern Orientalism', from the eighteenth century onwards, has created a stereotype of the gullible, untruthful, illogical, misogynistic, sexually insatiable, cruel and untrustworthy 'oriental' male, and of the passive female. According to Said:

> the principal dogmas of Orientalism exist in their purest form today in studies of the Arabs and Islam. Let us recapitulate them here: one is the absolute and systematic difference between the West, which is rational, developed, humane, superior, and the Orient, which is aberrant, undeveloped, inferior. Another dogma is that abstractions about the Orient, particularly those based on texts representing a 'classical' Oriental civilization, are always preferable to direct evidence drawn from modern Oriental realities. A third dogma is that the Orient is eternal, uniform, and incapable of defining itself; therefore it is assumed that a highly generalized and systematic vocabulary for describing the Orient from a Western standpoint is inevitable and even scientifically objective. A fourth dogma is that the Orient is at bottom something either to be feared (the Yellow peril, the Mongol hordes, the brown dominions) or to be controlled (by pacification, research and development, outright occupation wherever possible). (Said, *Orientalism*, 300f.)

In a series of later works, Said has extended and illustrated these basic points. His book, *Covering Islam* (1981), with its sub-title *How the Media and the Experts Determine how we See the Rest of the World*, emphasizes that his chief concern is with the West's attitude to Islam. One aspect of the West's misrepresentation of Islam is its slander of Muhammad and the Arabs. In *Orientalism*, Said cites a survey which highlighted the overwhelmingly defamatory treatment of Arabs and of Islam and its Prophet in American textbooks. One textbook quoted by the survey suggests that 'few people of this [Arab] area even know that there is a better way to live'. Another work suggests that 'the Moslem religion, called Islam, began in the seventh century. It was started by a wealthy businessman of Arabia, called Muhammad. He claimed that he was a prophet. He found followers among other Arabs. He told them that they were picked to rule the world' (quoted in Said, *Orientalism*, 287).

This misrepresentation of Muhammad and his followers builds upon the medieval Christian legacy of hatred for and fear of Muslims. Said reminds his readers of the Italian poet Dante's (1265–1321) treatment of Muhammad in canto 28 of the *Inferno*. Muhammad is placed in the eighth of the nine circles of hell. After him are only the falsifiers and the treacherous, including Judas Iscariot who betrayed Jesus.

Although Said defends Muhammad and Islam against misrepresentation by Christians and others, ironically, he is ignorant of much that is central to Islamic beliefs (and, incidentally and ironically, also of much in Christian faith). One example is his condemnation of the distinguished scholar Sir Hamilton Gibb, whom he calls 'the greatest name in modern Anglo-American Islamic studies' (Said, *Orientalism*, 53). Said faults Gibb for 'his assertion that the Islamic master science is law, which early on replaced theology'. In Said's view, this was an avowal 'made about Islam, not on the basis of evidence internal to Islam, but rather on the basis of a logic deliberately outside Islam' (ibid., 280). Yet Gibb was right. He was intent upon correcting the impressions of European students who conformed Islam's central concerns to Christianity's. Nor was it fair of Said to condemn Gibb for calling one of his books *Mohammedanism*, as though that were, in the opinion of Muslims, a correct synonym for Islam. Gibb's publishers insisted on this title, which was changed to the author's preferred designation, *Islam*, in a later edition.

The former Pakistani diplomat, thereafter Cambridge don, Akbar Ahmed, points out that

> However powerfully Said argues his case, the work of the older Orientalists was marked by many positive features. These included a lifetime's scholarship, a majestic command of languages, a wide vision and breadth of learning and an association with the established universities. (Ahmed, *Postmodernism and Islam*, 180)

Akbar Ahmed is right to point out that 'Said's Arab passion may have ultimately damaged his own cause. The *rite de passage*, the ritual slaying of the elders . . . , has been too noisy and too bloody' (ibid.).

Said is a passionate protestor. The holes in his argument are large and can easily be pointed out. Nevertheless, his polemic has served to remind his readers of the intricate and compromised relationships between the Western world and Islam. Unfortunately, they have also encouraged Muslims to dismiss as 'Orientalism' any critiques of aspects of Islam by Westerners. Orientalists write as outsiders and from particular perspectives, but that does not mean that their views are necessarily unconstructive, and that they write nothing that Muslims could profit by reading.

Muhammad *and* Christians

Negative medieval assessments of Muhammad by Christians have continued until recent times. Sir William Muir admired Muhammad's ministry in Makka. But, in his view:

> the scene changes at Medina. There temporal power, aggrandizement, and self-gratification mingled rapidly with the grand object of the Prophet's life [which was 'the idea of ONE great Being guiding with almighty power and wisdom all creation, and yet infinitely above it']; . . . Messages from heaven were freely brought down to justify political conduct in precisely the same manner as to inculcate religious precept. Battles were fought, executions ordered, and territories annexed, under cover of the Almighty's sanction. Nay, even personal indulgences were not only excused but encouraged by the divine approval or command. (Muir, *The Life of Mohammed*, 520, 518)

Muir wrote with more appreciation of certain aspects of the Prophet's life than many Muslims allow. But, at bottom, he was a passionate Christian, who regarded Muhammad as a man who had progressively allowed his deepest convictions to be overruled by personal desires; a man, too, whose inspiration may have come from illness or delusion rather than God. Indeed, most Christian scholars have been sceptical of Muhammad's integrity. A particular problem for them, stated or unstated, is that Islam is a post-Christian phenomenon. From their Christian perspective there is no need of another prophet after the coming of the Son of God; how can there be another religion after God's final self-revelation?

Contemporary Christian scholars still face these issues. Two of the most important of them are William Montgomery Watt and Kenneth Cragg (b.1913). Watt has made an important contribution to understanding the life of Muhammad in his two books *Muhammad at*

Mecca (1953) and *Muhammad at Medina* (1956). In a range of other books, he has also enlarged our understanding of early Islamic political thought, and furthered knowledge of many aspects of the history and thought of Islam.

Watt's major emphasis has not been on issues of inter-religious truth, but in reassessing information about the origin of Islam. He has portrayed Makka as a prosperous town, on important trade routes. This affluence created both *nouveaux riches* and an underclass of the economically disadvantaged. Along with this Marxist interpretation (now, as we have seen, overtaken by Crone's research) Watt argued, from a specifically Christian perspective, that Muhammad sincerely believed that he received revelation from God, even if we do not have to agree with the details of Muhammad's self-awareness.

In his biographies of the Prophet, Watt had been careful to write 'The Quran says', not, as Muslims believe, 'God says' or, so others claim, 'Muhammad says'. Towards the end of his later abridgement of his two-volume work, he asked:

> Was Muhammad a prophet? He was a man in whom creative imagination worked at deep levels and produced ideas relevant to the central questions of human existence, so that his religion has had a widespread appeal, not only in his own age but in succeeding centuries. Not all the ideas he produced are true and sound, but by God's grace he has been enabled to provide millions with a better religion than they had before they testified that there is no god but God and that Muhammad is the messenger of God (Watt, *Muhammad: Prophet and Statesman*, 240)

Much more recently, Watt reflected that:

> I always took the view – contrary to most previous scholars of Islam – that the Quran was not something Muhammad had consciously produced. For long, however, I hesitated to speak of him as a prophet, because Muslims would have taken this to mean that everything in the Quran was finally and absolutely true, which was something I did not believe. More recently, however, I have said that Muhammad is a prophet comparable to Old Testament prophets, though with a different task, namely, to bring the knowledge of God to people without such knowledge, whereas their task was mainly to criticize the conduct of those who already believed in God. (Forward, (ed.) *Ultimate Visions*, 283)

Watt's acceptance of Muhammad may encourage other Christians to view him in a more positive light than hitherto. Yet, as he admits, his interpretation is not how Muslims accept him. Analogously, many Muslims demand to know why Christians do not accept Muhammad as a prophet, when Islam grants that status to Jesus. They do not apprehend that Christian theology describes Jesus as a different sort of prophet to that described in the Quran, and also as more than a prophet (see chapter 3, pp. 66–72). It may not be enough to honour another's holy man, if the honouring subverts his most cherished meanings in the hearts and minds of those who believe differently.

That particular criticism could be levelled at Kenneth Cragg, who has written from a more openly Christian theological stance than Watt. His first book, *The Call of the Minaret*, looked at what Islam might mean for Muslims and also for Christians, and what Christian faith might mean for both. A significant sentiment in that book is recapitulated and developed in many other of Cragg's works:

> Part . . . of our Christian task . . . is patiently to dissipate the erroneous notion [of Muslims] that Christian theology is a piece of dispensable subtlety encumbering the simplicity of true theism. The Muslim needs to be awakened to the profundity of his own simplicities and the relevance of what he considers the Christian extravagances. Differences of view about God cannot properly be compared on the ground of comparative simplicity – not if He is truly their subject. The question must always be resolved into: How articulate is the simplicity? That question is only another way of asking: How adequately profound is the doctrine? (Cragg, *The Call of the Minaret*, 307)

This passage is found in a section headed 'The Call to Interpretation'. Cragg's works insist that Christians need to translate and clarify Christian theology, especially Gethsemane, Golgotha and the empty tomb, so that it can speak to Muslims as profoundly as it can to Christians. This implies that the Quran, or at least its interpreters, disavows and disallows what it does not truly understand. Just so, many Christians would say. But if Muslims were to do this, they would have to recognize the fallibility of their scripture. On this reading, the Quran would not only be a human document, but Muhammad would be a prophet who over-simplified the monotheistic vision and failed to do justice to the richness of the Christian doctrine of the atonement and Christianity's Trinitarian vision.

Cragg writes with subtlety and poetic vision. His books have to be carefully pondered and savoured for their full effect to be realized. Nevertheless, Islam would look very different if Muslims were convinced by his arguments.

It is crucially important that outsiders try to understand how Muslims feel when Christians and others apply the tools of modern scholarship to Islam, or exercise their own judgement about the value of Muhammad as a prophet. Even when the result is to some extent approving, the exercise seems to most Muslims to be inappropriate and patronizing at best, and blasphemous at worst. Long centuries of bitterness give credence to the view that this is the continuation of a Christian plot to discredit Islam. Although, in the last fifty years, British Christian scholars like Watt and Kenneth Cragg have been far more appreciative of Islam than many of their predecessors, many Muslims think that this admiration is the latest, more subtle trick of the Orientalists, undermining what it purports to admire.

Muhammad *and the* Unbelievers

Watt and Cragg question the truth and adequacy of aspects of Muhammad's vision of the one God. However, they do not doubt that it was his sincere desire to establish a community obedient to the dictates of the one God. The French Marxist and atheist, Maxime Rodinson, believes that Muhammad and they are mistaken in believing in the truth of a monotheistic revelation, though he does not seriously question Muhammad's integrity. In his biography of Muhammad, he develops Watt's Marxist theory of the origins of Islam, and even more his acceptance that the Prophet sincerely believed his call. Rodinson reckons that Muhammad's prophetic experiences can be explained, in the twentieth century, by 'modern advances in psychology and psychiatry' (Rodinson, *Muhammad*, 74).

There are others, however, who question Muhammad's integrity. One such has been Salman Rushdie. His novel, *The Satanic Verses* (London, Viking, 1988), brought down the wrath of the Ayatollah Khomeini and many other Muslims upon Rushdie's head, not least because he could be accused of *ridda* (apostasy; see chapter 3, pp. 61–2).

Rushdie's themes are of alienation and rootlessness, the plight of many humans, particularly those who are immigrant and urban, in a postmodern world. Although never a committed Muslim, Rushdie was born into a nominally Muslim family, so he naturally turned to the stories of Islam to construct his themes. His 'magic realism' transformed the form and meaning of these stories to describe the plight of contemporary humanness.

Rushdie's supporters admire the way in which his novels mock revered yet ambivalent institutions of the Western, post-enlightenment contemporary world, especially religious and political authority. These books refocus the range of possible interpretations and function of such institutions, to depict humanity's ultimate loneliness and the importance of the autonomy of the individual.

Most Muslims either cannot see the rich metamorphosis Rushdie effects, or else fundamentally disagree with it. Muslims accuse him of a slanderous misrepresentation of Islam to achieve his purpose in *The Satanic Verses*. The very title of the book picks up an event in the Prophet's life which can be used to question his integrity as the communicator of God's word rather than his own opinions (see chapter 2, pp. 34–5). Rushdie's Prophet-like figure is given the name Mahound, which medieval Christians polemicists used for Muhammad. He is a crook and a rogue, who fabricates revelation. His wives live in a harem that is little better than a brothel. Muslims see this as a new form of misrepresentation, dependent on the old Christian bigotry. Worse, in their view Rushdie is a lapsed Muslim who, unlike many Muslims, has made good in the West, and now affects to despise his religion.

Between Rushdie and his secular supporters, and the wrath and pain of traditional Muslims, lies an inability to empathize with, or sometimes even to understand, the other. Neither side seems willing to criticize its own position.

Rushdie is someone from a Muslim background who has become as sceptical of claims to religious truth as many nominal Christians. Muslims are not yet as willing as some Christians have become to stomach such an attack on their religious sensibilities. Rushdie and his friends hold fast to a postmodern criticism of authority, particularly revealed, religious authority. Yet they grant to their own liberalism, and to the novels they write or read, the enlightenment and influence they deny to others. They want others to see their liberalism as authoritative and normative. Others see it as more repressive than traditional religious authority.

History *and* Myth

Modern Western scholarship challenges the traditional tools of Muslim learning. A major difference between Muslim and modern Western scholars is in their understanding of history, and of God's action within it. The modern study of history rests on three major assumptions. First, history is the story of humanity's life on earth, as recorded in written and certain other materials that have survived through the process of time. Second, history is about meaning. As opposed to narrators or chroniclers who simply record the past, historians try to understand and interpret it, to unlock what it says about the human condition. Third, if historians are to understand the past, they need to recognize its 'otherness'. L. P. Hartley, in his novel *The Go-Between*, famously wrote: 'The past is a foreign country: they did things differently there.' If this is true of an individual's past, how much more true it is of the long, passing years of human history.

Of the three Western assumptions about history, Islam accepts that it is the story of people. It also agrees that it is a search for meaning, but here there are two deep chasms between Muslims and most Western historians. Unlike many Western historians, Islam has located that meaning in the one God, and regards his exclusion from the human quest as aberrant, indeed, as grotesque and shocking. Personally, I agree with Muslims on this point. However, I do not wholly agree with their ambivalent attitude towards myth as a tool to uncover meaning. Many Westerners regard religious beliefs as mythic. So, for them, more important than the certitude that the events in the life of Muhammad happened is what they mean in various strands of Islamic religious beliefs and practices. This importance lies partly in a sceptical attitude towards the belief that history is transmitted free from interpretative myth-making. It also rests on a conviction that the transformative power of myths can be observed and studied in its various effects on distinct cultures at different times.

Furthermore, with regard to the third assumption, Islam has assumed the fundamental solidarity of humankind across the ages, not the overwhelming mystery and strangeness of the past. This is illustrated by the fact that many Muslims live their lives as though the words and deeds of Muhammad can easily be translated into the context of twentieth-century attitudes and behaviour. For them, Muhammad is universally true, in every age and culture.

Yet Islam has changed in the past, and is still changing. Future intellectual changes may centre on a reinterpretation of central Muslim myths. If one were to define myth both as an interpretation of compelling and life-controlling power, and also, in its secondary sense, as containing elements not so much of a fairy-story as of a mismatch between belief, practice and observable reality, then several Islamic myths, in their present form, might need re-examination and reformulation. (One such myth in need of reinterpretation is that of a united *umma*, discussed in chapter 2.)

Many Muslims find it impossible to accept the idea of a rich symbiosis between myth and history, particularly when it is applied not only to the life of Muhammad but also to the status of the Quran. A sceptic, John Wansbrough holds that the Quran was developed amid Judaeo–Christian sectarian controversies and over a period of time up until the end of the eighth century. Thus, it was not boundaried by the Prophet's lifetime.[4] Other radical or sceptical Western scholars are also willing to question the Muslim belief in the integrity of the Quran. The traditional Muslim understanding is that the Quran was finally collected together when Uthman was caliph, about twenty years after the Prophet's death. Wansbrough and others hold that it was not set down until two centuries later, and that much material in it post-dates Muhammad, created to serve sectarian ends. Interestingly, another Western scholar has used sceptical methodology to draw a very different conclusion. John Burton believes that the Quran as we have it is the collection of Muhammad himself, put together in final form before his death.[5] Yet this conservative conclusion also diverges from the traditional Muslim view of an Uthmanic recension of the Quran.

Muslim and Western scholars differ greatly in answering the question, how is the Quran the word of God? This question raises three momentous issues. The first concerns the matter of the Prophet's involvement in the revelation. The second is the nature of the quranic language about revelation. The third is whether, in the modern, religiously plural world in which we live, another interpretation of the myth might serve Muslims and others better than the traditional one.

The vast majority of Muslims have believed that the Quran is the actual word of God:

4. Wansbrough, *Quranic Studies: Sources and Methods of Scriptural Interpretation.*
5. Burton, *The Collection of the Quran.*

Orthodox opinion has, from the earliest times, rigidly maintained that the illiterate prophet faithfully conveyed to his amanuensis the heavenly words that came to him, through Gabriel, taking scrupulous care not to confuse the inspired utterances with his own ordinary speech. The oral revelations preserved in the Koran are in fact, it is held, portions of a celestial speech whose original is inscribed on a guarded tablet in Heaven (K:85:22). The contra-natural descent of parts of this supernatural language marks a pivotal event in mortal history (K:97) completing Allah's gracious self-disclosure to men. The Koran in the original Arabic, safeguarded in Muslim memory and devotion, is therefore the literal and immutable word of Allah, infallibly dictated to his messenger and constituting the final and conclusive expression of the divine will in relationship to mankind. (Akhtar, *A Faith for all Seasons*, 40)

So writes Shabbir Akhtar, a British Muslim of Pakistani origin, in an admirable summary of the classic Muslim myth of revelation. In what form did Muhammad receive the revelation? Most Muslims have held that the Prophet was the passive recipient of an objective revelation. For example, the great historian, Ibn Khaldun (1332–1406) wrote that

The Quran is alone among the divine books, in that our Prophet received it directly in the words and phrases in which it appears. In this respect, it differs from the Torah, the Gospel and other heavenly books. The prophets received them in the form of ideas. (Rosenthal (trans.), *The Muqaddimah*, vol. 1, 192)

Other Muslim scholars have more clearly seen difficulties with this traditional doctrine, especially where history probes the assertions of myth. For an example of these difficulties: there was a somewhat complicated process of collecting the quranic text.[6] What are the implications of the length of this process, and the resultant variant texts, for the conviction that all the revealed words, neither more nor less, form the Quran as we now have it? However, the particular question under review here is the Prophet's involvement in the revelation. Akhtar writes that 'There cannot of course, for the committed Muslim, be two opinions about the authorship of the Islamic scripture.' In his view, either God or Muhammad must be the Quran's author, and he declares that 'I shall assume that these two possibilities are mutually exclusive: the Koran is not some amalgam of the divine and the human' (Akhtar, *A Faith for all Seasons*, 41).

---

6.   See Watt, *A Short History of Islam*, 48f. for a brief description.

A small number of Muslims have thought otherwise. In the middle and closing years of the nineteenth century, some Muslims in Egypt and British India began to update Islam, using modern Western methods and urging parents to educate their children in European languages. One such notable exponent was Syed Ameer Ali. He wrote these bold words about the idea of a future life in Islam:

> A careful study of the Koran makes it evident that the mind of Mohammed went through the same process of development which marked the religious consciousness of Jesus . . .
> The various chapters of the Koran which contain the ornate descriptions of paradise, whether figurative or literal, were delivered wholly or in part at Mecca. Probably in the infancy of his religious consciousness, Mohammed himself believed in some or other of the traditions which floated around him. But with a wider awakening of the soul, a deeper communion with the Creator of the Universe, thoughts, which bore a material aspect at first, became spiritualised. The mind of the Teacher progressed not only with the march of time and the development of his religious consciousness, but also with the progress of his disciples in apprehending spiritual conceptions. (Ali, *The Spirit of Islam*, 200f.)

It may be that Ameer Ali was propounding a view of the sole authorship by Muhammad of the Quran but, if so, it is extraordinary that he did not seem to realize the singular and unorthodox nature of his conviction. It is more likely that he was trying, rather clumsily and simplistically, and with too much reliance on nineteenth-century European notions of the progressive development of humankind, to restate orthodox views in ways that his audience could appreciate and affirm. However, he failed crucially to describe *how* God speaks his word through the Prophet.

A more modern and subtle attempt to find some space for Muhammad in the revelation given by God to him and then through him, is that of Fazlur Rahman (1919–87):

> The moral law and religious values are God's Command, and although they are not identical with God entirely, they are part of Him. The Quran is, therefore, purely divine. Further, even with regard to ordinary consciousness, it is a mistaken notion that ideas and feelings float about in it and can be mechanically 'clothed' in words. There exists, indeed, an organic relationship between feelings, ideas and words. In inspiration, even in poetic inspiration, this relationship is so complete that feeling-idea-word is a total complex with a life of its own. When

> Muhammad's moral intuitive perception rose to the highest point
> and became identified with the moral law itself . . . , the Word
> was given with the inspiration itself. The Quran is thus pure
> Divine Word, but, of course, it is equally intimately related to the
> inmost personality of the Prophet Muhammad whose relationship
> to it cannot be mechanically conceived like that of a record. The
> Divine Word flowed through the Prophet's heart. (Rahman,
> *Islam*, 32f.)

Fazlur Rahman, too, failed to answer the question he raised, or to
convince many Muslims to agree with him. His views were widely
condemned in Pakistan, and he left, spending his last years teaching in
the USA.

So Shabbir Akhtar's assertion represents the myth of revelation
as it is held by nearly all Muslims. From a non-Muslim perspective,
where this traditional form of the myth could be said to fall short of
complete credibility is precisely in making Muhammad a cipher
with regard to the primary revelation of the Quran, yet wholly
crucial to the secondary revelation of the *hadith*. Muslims have
argued that the myth is coherent: the Quran upholds both the
traditional view of its divine origin and the Prophet's passive
receptivity of it (Q17.105f.) on the one hand and, on the other, his
role as a model for believers (Q33.21). However, the point at issue
is not its coherence but, rather, its relevance and flexibility. The
usual form of the myth makes perfect sense of certain quranic
verses. But does it make sense of the contemporary world in which
Muslims live? And is it the only way in which quranic material can
be interpreted?

The question of how quranic material is to be read was widely and
controversially discussed in the early Islamic centuries. One otherwise
diverse group, the Mutazila, held two views which were later regarded
as unorthodox: the createdness of the Quran; and an allegorical
attitude to the physical attributes of God mentioned in the Quran.
Their convictions are known only through their opponents (their name
means 'seceders'), and so must be treated very cautiously, but they
seem to have held that belief in an uncreated Quran compromised
tawhid, the unity of God. In their view, if the Quran was not created by
God, but had always coexisted with him, then that seemed like *shirk*,
associating something else with God, as God.[7] In the end their views
were rejected and those of a former member, al-Ashari (873/4–935/6),

7. There were other, especially political, implications behind the 'theological'
   differences between the Mutazila and their opponents. See Watt, *Islamic
   Philosophy and Theology*, 58–71.

prevailed. He came to believe that quranic anthropomorphisms about God, such as references to his face, must be accepted *bila qayf*, 'without knowing how'.

Sunni orthodoxy has held these views ever since. There are at least two problems with them. First, logically, the Mutazila were right that the doctrine of an uncreated Quran sits ill with an uncompromising monotheism. Secondly, *bila qayf* is a device which creates more problems than it solves. Specifically, what does it mean to talk of God's face without knowing how? It renders part of God's revelation beyond the power of humans to understand, when the Quran calls itself 'the book that makes things clear' (Q43.2).

There are hints that the earliest Muslims, although respectful of the divine word, were willing to engage with it in more creative ways than the simple acceptance and unquestioning obedience which many contemporary Muslims claim to hold. When Muhammad died, Abu Bakr quoted a quranic verse: 'Muhammad is nothing more than a Messenger. Many have been the messengers who died before him. If he died or were slain, would you then turn back upon your heels?' (Q3.144). Some observers were puzzled, and claimed that they had not heard this verse before. Did Abu Bakr remember it as carefully as proponents of the theory that the Quran is as it came from God, maintain? A more radical, even shocking, view would be that he made it up, as a creative way of convincing the Muslim community that the death of the Prophet was not the end of Islam.

Of course, many non-Muslims are deeply sceptical about the convenience of some of the verses which relate to Muhammad's marriages, and few are persuaded by traditional Muslim explanations of the Quran's origins. In the wider field of Religious Studies, many Christian and Jewish scholars, although they greatly respect the power and authority of scripture (other people's scriptures, as well as their own), raise issues about the origin of their own sacred texts which very few Muslims have felt able to raise about the Quran. For these scholars it has been a liberating experience to find the word of God in the words of human beings. Could Muslims? What difference would it make to deal, not with the myth of revelatory certainties, but with the less unequivocal disciplines of historical and other modern scholarships?

Some Western scholars hold that it is only a matter of time before Muslims will be forced to study their past with tools forged in the enlightenment and the postmodern West. Others are not so sure. To this latter group, it seems a kind of parochial arrogance to elevate the intellectual tools of one area of the globe, and from one small part of its history, as the fit vehicles for all people everywhere to understand the truth of things. Furthermore, Muslims have been extraordinarily resistant to the demands of outsiders that they must change according to a new and alien agenda. This has not been simple bloody-mindedness on the part of Muslim scholars. To an extent, Islam appeals to many Westerners for whom modernism and postmodernism are godless cul-de-sacs. It is one of the fastest growing religions in the world today, maybe precisely because it values and conserves the past, and is suspicious of change as *bida*, or godless innovation.

Muhammad *in* Muslim Estimation

Most recent Muslims are either unaware of or deeply antagonistic towards the assumptions, which they might interpret as presumptions, of sceptical Western scholars. Yet these Muslims depict Muhammad as the solution to the problems of a world that is quite different from the classical period of Islam.

The early biographer, Ibn Ishaq, had no difficulty with the miracles associated with Muhammad. He recorded wondrous stories from Muhammad's infancy: Muhammad's foster-mother's sheep always had milk when she was suckling him; two men in white split his belly and washed his heart and innards with snow. The mature Muhammad emerges from his account as a warrior leader and a lover of women. Ibn Ishaq saw all these endowments as virtues, illustrations of his subject's heroic status and numinous qualities.

Modern virtues are often more austere and sober. Hence, many Muslim scholars of the last century have located Muhammad's greatness not in the miracles which surround his life, nor in his military prowess and remarkable relations with women, but in his role in the transformation of society. One of them was Syed Ameer Ali. His convictions are reflected in the title of his most important work: the life and teachings of Muhammad illustrate *The Spirit of Islam*. That spirit is more important than the dead letter of scholastic theology, or mystic endeavour, or speculative philosophy. It also exalts rationalism over the miraculous:

Disclaiming every power of wonder-working, the Prophet of Islam ever rests the truth of his divine commission entirely upon his Teachings. He never resorts to the miraculous to assert his influence or to enforce his warnings. He invariably appeals to the familiar phenomena of nature as signs of the divine presence. He unswervingly addresses himself to the inner consciousness of man, to his reason, and not to his weakness or his credulity. (Ali, *The Spirit of Islam*, 32f.)

In Ameer Ali's view, only as Islam follows the spirit of Muhammad in aiming for continual human progress will it truly flourish and recapture its essential purpose. Although his writings have a certain allure, the two world wars since his death in 1928 have tarnished the optimistic and somewhat theoretical liberalism he advocated.

Differences exist between Muslim scholars, past and present, about the exact or even general importance of Muhammad. Nevertheless they are at one in stressing that his life *is* crucially important for Muslim faith. Again, Ameer Ali testified that

A nature so pure, so tender, and yet so heroic, inspires not only reverence, but love . . . His courteousness to the great, his affability to the humble, and his dignified bearing to the presumptuous, procured him universal respect and admiration. His countenance reflected the benevolence of his heart . . . His singular elevation of mind, his extreme delicacy of feeling, his purity and truth, form the constant theme of the traditions. He was most indulgent to his inferiors, and would never allow his awkward little page to be scolded whatever he did . . . Those who saw him were suddenly filled with reverence; those who came near him loved him; they who described him would say, 'I have never seen his like, either before or after'. (Ibid., 118ff.)

Many years before, from the infancy of Islam, Ibn Ishaq quotes one Hassan, a contemporary of the Prophet who, mourning Muhammad's death, said that

By God, no woman has conceived and given birth
To one like the apostle the prophet and guide of his people;
Nor has God created among his creatures
One more faithful to his sojourner or his promise
Than he who was the source of our light,
Blessed in his deeds, just, and upright . . .
O best of men, I was as it were in a river
Without which I have become lonely in my thirst.
(Guillaume, *The Life of Muhammad*, 690)

Muhammad's status among all Muslims is assured. By them, he is regarded with deepest veneration and love. He is, according to their scripture, which they reverence as the precise word of God, 'the seal of the Prophets' (Q.33.40), the last in a long line which stretches back to Adam, the first man, and includes Abraham, Moses, David and Jesus. He brought the climactic scripture, which confirms but also purifies previous revelations to the Jews, Christians and others. As people obey God's will enshrined in the Quran, they discover that they are creatures destined for eternity, not bound and destroyed by time.

What manner of man, then, was he? Proponents of a traditional attitude to the sources for Muhammad's life can conjure up a picture of his appearance as an adult. He was of average height or a little taller. He was strongly built. His complexion was fair. He had a hooked nose, and black eyes flecked with brown. He had a good head of hair, and was bearded. He had a large mouth, which occasionally broke into a warm smile. His was a mobile body: he turned his whole self to look at someone, spoke rapidly and to the point, and was often in a rush.

His physical appearance is less important than his spiritual qualities. Although Islam condemns the Christian notion of incarnation, on the grounds that God alone is God whilst human beings, however important, are human beings, Muhammad is considered closest of all people to God. In the mosque, the place of communal prayers, and on plaques and ornaments in Muslim homes, Arabic calligraphy conjoins Muhammad's name with that of God. Every year, on Muhammad's birthday, festivities begin and poems are recited in his honour. His name is never mentioned without prefacing it with the designation 'The Prophet', and following it with the suffix, *Salla Allah alayhi wa sallam*, 'May God bless him and grant him peace', or some similar translation. Muslims remember what he said and did as normative words and behaviour for all, so that, for example, his life is studied to discover what to eat, wear, or what to say in particular circumstances. When my Arabic teacher, long years ago in India, spoke of Muhammad to me, tears of joy flowed into his white beard, and his face became radiant. No wonder, then, that when Christians and secularists lampoon Muhammad, Muslims are angry and upset; still more when it is one of their own, like Salman Rushdie.

Shabbir Akhtar underlines what he calls 'the posthumous authority of Muhammad':

> Muhammad is unique in the respect and honour afforded him by his
> followers. Though not regarded as divine, Muhammad is held in the

highest possible esteem . . . The influence of the Arabian Prophet on the lives of millions, through the patterns of his biography daily imitated, is without parallel in the whole of history, religious or secular. The imitation of Muhammad is, unlike the imitation of Christ, an accepted obligation, a routine occurrence. It is the ideal not only for the saints – but for all Muslims, from the beggars in the slums of India to the spectacularly wealthy sheikhs of Saudi Arabia . . . Muhammad is dead. But he is dead only in the least significant sense. For he is ideologically alive – and well. (Akhtar, *Be Careful with Muhammad!*, 2f.)

Muhammad: A Personal Estimate

What of Muhammad's status for non-Muslims? In the religiously diverse world in which we live, Muhammad can no more be a universally revered figure than any other religious leader. They each have their own devotees, but also their detractors. Muhammad is held in suspicion by many Christians, feminists, and others. He is regarded as irrelevant by most atheists.

However, scholars of Religious Studies naturally ask about questions of religious truth. They do so from a particular perspective: that religion is a crucially important phenomena for forming and motivating the beliefs and practices of humankind. Having examined a small range of the many non-Muslim views about Muhammad, I end with a personal assessment of him.

The traditional Muslim, indeed quranic, estimation that Muhammad is the seal of the prophets, is not the view from my own Christian perspective, when it is interpreted to mean that Muhammad was the last and greatest of the prophets sent to the various *umma*s of humankind. Not only the religion I hold, but the Western historiographical and other academic tools in which I have been trained, predispose me to look at issues of revelation, prophetic authority and the origins of religion very differently from Muslims. I do so not only in relation to Islam but also towards other religions, including Christianity. Nevertheless, I deplore the Christian polemic against Muhammad, widespread in former eras, which still is to be found in our own times. Although much of this is explicable on historical and other grounds, even so, those who seek to cast lustre upon their own religion by darkening another do themselves and their faith little honour and less justice.

I have argued in chapter 3, in relation to quranic estimations of Jesus, that religions use commonly held honorific titles to very different ends. Thus, when Muslims call Jesus the Messiah, or deny that he is the Son of God, this does not carry weight with Christians, who understand these titles very differently from Muhammad, the Quran and Muslims. Hence, I do not find the attempts by Watt and others to deem Muhammad a prophet very convincing, although I applaud their attempts to seek a positive, even an honoured role for him in Christian as well as Muslim estimation. The problem is that the concept of prophecy is quite dissimilar in Islam and Christianity. Muslims and Christians deceive themselves when they think that, by calling Muhammad a prophet, they mean the same or even a comparable thing.

My own estimation of Muhammad begins elsewhere, in the deep respect I have for the integrity and quality of lives demonstrated by many Muslim friends. They regard the good they do as directly emanating from their obedience to the law of God, manifest in the life of Muhammad. Although I may regard him quite differently from Muslims, I do not doubt that God has used their convictions about him to empower and enlighten them. The fact that his life gives their life meaning has led me to examine it. As an outsider, and from my own limited perspective, I have found myself puzzled and far from attracted by some incidents in his life (though these may have been exaggerated by those who recorded his exploits in an age whose virtues were quite different from our own). More often, however, I have been impressed and moved by his intuitive insight into the human condition, his empathy for others, his political and human skills, his ethical endeavours, and above all by his commitment to the will of the one God for his creation, especially his human servants.

Indeed, the genius of Islam has been to enshrine Muhammad's ideal of a single human community in which political, social and economic matters are held together as the will of the one God for humankind. Since this is a fascinating, alluring and contentious issue, it follows that Muhammad remains a fascinating, alluring and contentious figure for more than just Muslims. He is so for me: this much at least I can, in admiration, say about Muhammad, the man of God who has made God real for millions of people over many centuries.

Glossary

ahl al-kitab
'People of the Book', Jews and Christians

ansar
'helpers',
the first followers of Muhammad

bida
godless innovation

dhimmi
non-Muslim communities living under Muslim protection

hadith
an oral tradition describing a deed or saying of the Prophet

hajj
pilgrimage to Makka

hanif
follower of the monotheist religion of Abraham

hijab
veil

hijra
Muhammad's emigration from Makka to Madina

Imam
one of the twelve religious leaders recognized by Shia Muslims

Ismailis
a branch of Shia Islam

jahiliyya
'the age of ignorance' before Islam

jihad
struggle in God's cause

jizya
tax

Kaba
sacred building in Makka

khalifa
caliph, political leader of the Muslims

maghazi
raiding campaigns

muhajirun
'emigrants', those who emigrated to Madina with Muhammad

munafiqun
hypocrites

nabi
prophet

rasul
messenger of God

ridda
apostasy

salat
ritual prayer

sawm
fasting during Ramadan

shahada
the profession of Muslim faith

Sharia
Muslim religious law

Shia
Muslims who adhere to the claims of Ali and his successors to lead the Muslim community

sira
a biography of Muhammad

Sufism
Islam's main mystical tradition

Sunni
the majority group within Islam

sura
a chapter of the Quran

umma
the Muslim community

umra
minor pilgrimage to Makka

zakat
almsgiving

Bibliography

Chapter 1

Ali, S. A., *The Spirit of Islam*. London, Chatto & Windus, 1922

Guillaume, A., *The Life of Muhammad: A Translation of Ibn Ishaq's 'Sirat Rasul Allah'*. London, Oxford University Press, 1955

Watt, W. M., *Muhammad at Medina*. Edinburgh, Edinburgh University Press, 1956

— *Muhammad: Prophet and Statesman*. London, Oxford University Press, 1961

Chapter 2

Ali, S. A., *The Spirit of Islam*. London, Chatto & Windus, 1922

Baldick, J., *Mystical Islam*. London, I. B. Tauris, 1989

Nicholson, R. A. (trans.), *Rúmí: Poet and Mystic*. Oxford, Oneworld, 1995

Robson, J. (trans.), *Mishkat al-masabih*, vol. 1. Lahore, Muhammad Ashraf, 1981

Watt, W. M., *A Short History of Islam*. Oxford, Oneworld, 1996

Chapter 3

Ahmed, A., *Living Islam*. London, BBC Books, 1993
Ahmed, A. S., *Postmodernism and Islam*. London, Routledge, 1992
Ali, A. Y., *The Holy Quran: Text, Translation and Commentary*. Leicester, The Islamic Foundation, 1975
Ali, S. A., *The Spirit of Islam*. London, Chatto & Windus, 1922
Daniel, N., *Islam and the West: The Making of an Image*. Oxford, Oneworld, 1997
Hussein, K., *City of Wrong* (trans. K. Cragg). London, Godfrey Bles, 1959
Parrinder, G., *Jesus in the Quran*. Oxford, Oneworld, 1995

Chapter 4

Ali, S. A., *A Critical Examination of the Life and Teachings of Mohammed*. London, Williams and Norgate, 1873
— *The Spirit of Islam*. London, Chatto & Windus, 1922
Mernissi, F., *Women and Islam: An Historical and Theological Enquiry*, trans. M. J. Lakeland. Oxford, Blackwell, 1991
— *The Veil and the Male Elite*. Reading, Addison-Wesley, 1991
Muir, W., *The Life of Mohammed*, revised T. H. Weir. Edinburgh, John Grant, 1923
Spellberg, D. A., *Politics, Gender, and the Islamic Past: The Legacy of 'A'isha bint Abi Bakr*. New York, Columbia, 1994

Chapter 5

Ahmed, A. S., *Postmodernism and Islam*. London, Routledge, 1992
Akhtar, S., *Be Careful with Muhammad!* London, Bellew, 1989
— *A Faith For All Seasons: Islam and Western Modernity*. London, Bellew, 1990
Burton, J., *The Collection of the Quran*. Cambridge, Cambridge University Press, 1977
Clarke, P. (ed.), *The World's Religions: Islam*. London, Routledge, 1990
Cragg, K., *The Call of the Minaret*. Oxford, Oxford University Press, 1956
Crone, P., *Meccan Trade and the Rise of Islam*. Princeton, Princeton University Press, 1987
Crone, P. and Cook, M. *Hagarism*. Cambridge, Cambridge University

Press, 1977

Forward, M. (ed.), *Ultimate Visions*. Oxford, Oneworld, 1995

Goldziher, I., *Muslim Studies*, 2 vols. London, George Allen & Unwin, 1968 [originally published 1889, 1890]

Guillaume, A., *The Life of Muhammad: A Translation of Ibn Ishaq's 'Sirat Rasul Allah'*. London, Oxford University Press, 1955

Muir, W., *The Life of Mohammed*, revised T. H. Weir. Edinburgh, John Grant, 1923

Rahman, F., *Islam*. Chicago, The University of Chicago Press, 1979

Rosenthal, F. (trans.), *The Muqaddimah*, vol. 1. London, Routledge & Kegan Paul, 1967

Said, E., *Orientalism*. London, Peregrine, 1985

Schacht, J., *The Origins of Muhammadan Jurisprudence*. Oxford, Clarendon Press, 1950

Wansbrough, J., *Quranic Studies: Sources and Methods of Scriptural Interpretation*. Oxford, Oxford University Press, 1977

— *The Sectarian Milieu: Content and Composition of Islamic Salvation History*. Oxford, Oxford University Press, 1978

Watt, W. M., *Islamic Philosophy and Theology*. Edinburgh, Edinburgh University Press, 1962

— *Muhammad: Prophet and Statesman*. London, Oxford University Press, 1961

— *Muslim–Christian Encounters: Perceptions and Misperceptions*. London, Routledge, 1991

— *A Short History of Islam*. Oxford, Oneworld, 1995

Further Reading

Ahmad, B., *Muhammad and the Jews: A Re-Examination*. New Delhi, Vikas, 1979

Ahmed, A. S., *Discovering Islam: Making Sense of Muslim History and Society*. London, Routledge, 1988

Ahmed, L., *Women and Gender in Islam*. New Haven, Yale University Press, 1992

Ali, A. (trans.), *Sacred Writings, Islam: The Quran*. New York, Quality Paperback Book Club, 1992

Arkoun, M., *Rethinking Islam: Common Questions, Uncommon Answers*. Boulder, San Francisco and Oxford, Westview, 1994

Bowker, J., *Voices of Islam*. Oxford, Oneworld, 1995

Burton, J., *An Introduction to the Hadith*. Edinburgh, Edinburgh University Press, 1994

Cook, M., *Muhammad*. Oxford, Oxford University Press, 1983

Doi, A. R. I., *Non-Muslims under Sharia (Islamic Law)*. London, Ta-Ha, 1983

Endres, G., *An Introduction to Islam*. Edinburgh, Edinburgh University Press, 1988

Gätje, H., *The Quran and its Exegesis*. Oxford, Oneworld, 1996

Lewis, B. (ed.), *The World of Islam: Faith, People, Culture*. London,

Thames & Hudson, 1976

Murata, S. and Chittick, W. C., *The Vision of Islam*. London and New York, I. B. Tauris, 1996

Nasr, S. H. (ed.), *Islamic Spirituality: Manifestations*. London, SCM, 1991

Nasr, S. H. and Leaman, O. (eds), *History of Islamic Philosophy*, Parts 1 and 2. London and New York, Routledge, 1996

Peters, R., *Jihad in Classical and Modern Islam*. Princeton, Markus Wiener, 1996

Phipps, W. E., *Muhammad and Jesus*. London, SCM, 1996

Rahman, F., *Islam and Modernity*. Chicago, University of Chicago Press, 1984

— *Major Themes of the Quran*. Minneapolis, Bibliotheca Islamica, 1989

Richard, Y., *Shiite Islam*. Oxford, Blackwell, 1995

Rippin, A., *Muslims: Their Religious Beliefs and Practices*. Volume 1, *The Formative Period*. London, Routledge, 1990

Robinson, N., *Discovering the Quran: A Contemporary Approach to a Veiled Text*. London, SCM, 1996

Rodinson, M., *Muhammad*, trans. A. Carter. 2nd English edition, London, Penguin, 1996

Schimmel, A., *And Muhammad is his Messenger*. Chapel Hill, University of North Carolina Press, 1985

— *Mystical Dimensions of Islam*. Chapel Hill, University of North Carolina Press, 1975

Stowasser, B. F., *Women in the Quran, Traditions, and Interpretation*. New York, Oxford University Press, 1994

Watt, W. M., *The Influence of Islam on Medieval Europe*. Edinburgh, Edinburgh University Press, 1972

— *Muslim–Christian Encounters: Perceptions and Misperceptions*. London, Routledge, 1991

Index

Abd al-Muttalib 9, 15
Abd Shams 14, 73
Abraham 10–11, 16, 32–3, 44, 50, 55, 56, 71, 100, 118
Abu Bakr 7, 12, 14, 17, 39, 40, 44, 83, 88, 90, 93, 115
Abu Hanifa 61
Abu Hudhayfa 24
Abu Hurayra 91–2
Abu Sufyan 23, 24, 27, 29, 30, 73
Abu Talib 9, 14, 15
Abyssinia 15, 28, 35, 36, 83
adultery 80, 89, 92
Ahmadiyya movement 63, 68
Ahmed, Akbar 75, 104
Aisha 7, 36, 61, 77, 83, 84, 88–94
Akhtar, Shabbir 112, 114, 118–19
Ali 11, 39, 40–1, 42, 74, 90–2
Ali, Karamat Syed 61
Ali, Syed Ameer 18, 26, 41, 62, 80, 81, 82, 92, 93, 94–5, 113, 116–17
Ali, Yusuf 60, 63
alms (zakat) 20, 38, 59, 88
apostasy (ridda) I, 59, 61–2, 75, 108

Aquinas, T. 65
Arabia 1, 2, 7, 8, 9, 10, 17, 29, 30, 33, 54, 64, 74, 76, 86, 101, 103
Aristotle 65
Atatürk, Mustafa Kemal 74

Badr, Battle of 23, 27, 74, 84
Bahai Faith 63
Baldick, J. 47, 100, 101, 102
Bangladesh 74
Bhutto, Benazir 96
Bilal 14, 29
birth 12, 49–50, 52, 70, 78
Bosnia 64
Buath, Battle of 17
Buddha 3, 62
Buddhism 62, 72
burial 50

caliphs 3, 12, 15, 30, 40, 41, 73–4, 84, 92, 93, 111; rightly-guided (rashidun) 39, 41, 73
Camel, Battle of the 90, 92
Christianity 2, 9, 11, 12, 30, 32, 54–8,

64–73, 105–8
circumcision 50, 77, 96: female 77, 96
clans 9–10, 14–19, 21, 23, 73–4, 90
Constantine, Emperor 64
Constantinople 64, 75
Cook, M. 99, 100
Cragg, K. 68, 105, 107, 108
Crone, P. 99, 100, 101, 106
Crusades 65

Dante, A. 104
death 2, 10, 12, 13, 15, 46, 49, 50
dhimmi 28
Ditch, Battle of the 25, 28
divorce 61, 80, 81, 84, 85, 87
dowries 79–80, 82

Eve 78

Fatima 10, 40, 41, 88
five pillars of Islam 38, 59
fundamentalism 61
funeral rites 50

Gabriel (Jibril) 3, 11, 20, 23, 33, 34,
    44, 45, 88, 112
Gethsemane 107
al-Ghazali, Abu Hamid Muhammad
    46–7
Ghulam Ahmad, Mirza 63
Gibb, Sir H. 104
God: *see* monotheism, prophecy,
    Quran, Muhammad
Goldziher, I. 99
Gregory VII, Pope 65

hadith 3, 20, 35, 37–8, 43–4, 51, 61,
    78, 80, 86–7, 91–2, 93, 95, 98–9,
    102, 114; *nabawi* 38; *qudsi* 38, 44
Hafsa 83
Hamza 15, 24, 27
Hashim 14, 15
heaven 2, 13, 22, 31, 33, 44–5, 59, 79,
    93, 105, 112
hell 12, 13, 15, 31, 32, 39, 53, 57, 104
hijra 5, 17, 18, 19–20, 22, 100
Hijaz
Hind 27, 28, 29
Hinduism 62, 63

Holy Land 100
homosexuality 48
Hudaybiyya, Treaty of 29
human rights 26, 77
Hussein, K. 68–9
al-hutama 57

Ibn Abd al-Wahhab 50
ibn Amr, Suhayl 29
Ibn Hisham 3, 35, 38, 101
Ibn Ishaq 3, 35, 38, 101, 116, 117
Ibn Khaldun 112
ibn Rabia, Utba 24, 27
Ibn Rushd 65
Ibn Sad 86
ibn Sulayman, Muqatil 45
ibn Ubayy, Abdallah 19, 24, 25, 89
ibn Walid, Khalid 25, 29, 30
idolatry 10, 11, 12–13, 16, 24, 29, 36,
    56
India 8, 61, 63, 74, 84, 113, 118, 119
inheritance 20, 37, 61, 81
Inter-Faith Network 63
Internet 76
Iscariot, Judas 67, 104
Ishmael 32, 33, 100
Ismailis 42
isnad 37
Israel 55, 56

Jamaat-I-Islami 96
Jerusalem 30, 43, 44, 64, 56, 68, 100
Jesus 3, 11, 12, 29, 44, 46, 54, 57, 62,
    64, 66–72, 78, 88, 93, 95, 101,
    104, 107, 113, 118, 120; Jesus as
    prophet 69, 107
Jibril *see* Gabriel
jihad (struggle) 59–60, 75
Jinnah, Fatima 96
Jinnah, Muhammad Ali 96
jizya (tax) 28, 62, 75
Judaism 9, 11, 12, 16–17, 19, 24–5, 28,
    30, 32, 45, 53, 54–9, 62, 63, 65, 66,
    67–8, 69, 71, 76, 91, 100, 115, 118

Kaba 8, 9, 13, 16, 29, 33, 44, 55
Karbala, Battle of 40
Khadija 10, 11, 15, 36, 83–4, 88, 92–3

Khan, Sir S. A. 68, 98
Khomeini, Ayatollah 108

Laroui, Abdallah 102
al-Lat 10, 14, 34
laza 57

Madina 5, 15, 17–28, 30, 36, 37, 44,
    51, 54, 55, 56–9, 61, 66, 69, 76,
    84, 87, 88–90, 91, 95, 100
Makka 5, 8–9, 10, 11–15, 16–25, 27–9,
    30, 32–8, 40, 43, 44, 46, 59, 60,
    61, 69, 73, 74, 79, 83, 100, 105, 106
Manat 10, 34
Mariya the Copt 33, 83, 86, 87, 92
marriage 15, 20, 37, 49, 61, 77, 79–81,
    82–94, 115
Martel, C. 64
Mary 29, 44, 67, 70, 78, 88
matn 38
Mernissi, Fatima 91, 95, 96, 99
messengers 7, 13–14, 21, 29, 30, 31–2,
    34, 49, 56, 59, 62, 67, 69–70, 106,
    112, 115
miracles 45, 116
Mirza Ali Muhammad 63
monasticism 49
monotheism 12–13, 15, 16, 30, 32, 33,
    54, 56, 57, 58, 100, 115; Arabian 33,
    54, 56
Moses 11, 13, 44, 47, 62, 63, 71, 118
mosques 14, 20, 22, 33, 34, 43, 51, 60,
    75, 92, 118
muhajirun (emigrants) 18–19, 22, 24,
    25, 35, 83, 88, 100
Muhammad: and Abraham 32–3; as
    community leader 17–21, 43; death
    of 7, 13, 30, 39, 40, 59, 76; as
    defender of the faith 59–63; as
    intercessor 52; and Jesus 66–72, 107;
    life of 9–30; marriages of 10, 17, 77,
    82, 83–93, 115; and mysticism 43,
    45; as political leader 30, 35, 39,
    63–6, 76; as prophet 8–17, 29–30,
    31–6, 39, 44, 48, 55, 56, 59, 61, 62,
    70, 103, 119; as warrior leader 21–8,
    116
Muir, Sir W. 84, 86, 90, 105
muslim 11, 31, 32, 50

muta 82
Mutazila 114–15
mysticism 32, 42–3, 45–7, 50, 63, 71,
    116; see also Sufi Islam
myth 4, 41, 74, 110–16

Netton, I. 4

Orientalists 102–5, 108

paganism 10, 11, 12, 13, 20, 22, 23, 33,
    54, 60, 61, 76
Pakistan 63, 74–5, 96, 100, 104, 112,
    113
Parrinder, G. 1, 68–9, 71
People of the Book (*ahl al-kitab*) 55, 62,
    67
pilgrimage (*hajj*) 16, 22, 28–9, 38, 40,
    46, 59
Poiters, Battle of 64
polygamy 77, 82–3, 84, 86, 94, 97
polygyny *see* polygamy
prayer 20, 37, 38, 50–2, 59, 62, 118; *see
    also* salat
prayer-beads (*subha*) 50
prophecy 31–2, 44, 45, 50, 63, 69, 70,
    72, 120; *see also* Jesus, Muhammad
prophet(s) 31–2, 44, 45, 50, 63, 69;;
purda 87

al-Qaim, Muhammad 42
Qaynuqa 17, 24
Quran 4, 8, 10–11, 15, 23, 37, 38,
    50–1, 63, 98, 102, 106: and apostasy
    61; and Christianity 54–9, 66–76,
    107, 120; exegesis 42, 57, 114; and
    jihad 59–60; and Judaism 54–9, 69;
    and monotheism 10–12, 15, 27,
    32–3; origin/revelation of 3, 13, 20,
    33–6, 38, 98, 99, 111-15;
    integrity/status of 3, 33–6, 98–9,
    111–15; and the prophecy of
    Muhammad 31–3; teachings 13,
    19–20, 22, 25, 26–7, 37, 52, 80–8;
    and women 77–96
Quraysh 9, 14, 16, 18, 19, 21, 23, 24,
    25, 27, 28, 34–5, 40, 73, 74, 76,
    90, 95
Qurayza 17, 25–6, 55

130

Rahman, Fazlur 113, 114
raid (*razzia*) 8, 21, 22–3, 26, 27, 99
Ramadan 20, 33, 38, 55, 59
religious law *see Sharia*
revelation 7, 9, 11, 12, 21, 22, 30, 33,
    34–5, 36, 38, 39, 40, 43, 48, 55,
    58, 59, 69, 71, 72, 78, 87, 88, 89, 90,
    93, 95, 99, 105, 106,   108, 109,
    111, 112, 113, 114–15, 118, 119; *see
    also* Quran
ridda (apostasy) 59, 61, 62
rites of passage 49–50
Rodinson, M. 100, 101, 108
Roman Empire 30, 64
Rumi, Jalal al-Din 47–9
Rushdie, S. I, 76, 108–9, 118

Said, E. 103–4
salat (prayers) 20, 59
Salih 14, 32
Satan 12, 34, 35, 66, 78, 88
Satanic Verses 34, 35, 36
Satanic Verses, The 76, 108–9
Sauda 83, 84
sawm (fasting) 59; *see also* Ramadan
Schacht, J. 99
scholarship 3, 8, 14, 39, 57, 61, 67,
    72–73, 83, 98, 104, 108, 115, 119;
    Christian 84, 105–8, 115; Jewish 115;
    Muslim 3, 10, 12, 18, 39, 49, 60–1,
    67, 75, 83, 100, 106, 112, 116, 117;
    Western 3, 5, 21, 35, 39, 77, 84,
    98–102, 108, 110, 111, 116
shahada 49, 50, 59
Shams al-Din 47
Sharia 19–20, 38, 39, 40, 42, 77,
    78–83, 91; and women 78–83
Shia Islam 10, 40–2, 43, 52, 73, 76, 82,
    92, 94
shrines 8, 29, 52
Siffin, Battle of 41
Sikhism 63
Simon of Cyrene 67
Spain 56, 64, 65, 75
Sufi Islam 42–9, 52, 66, 71
Sunni Islam 37–9, 40, 41, 42, 43, 46,
    48, 49, 52, 73, 74, 76, 88, 91, 92,
    93, 115

Tabari 3, 34, 35, 67, 84
tashahhud 12
Throne Verse 52
Trinity 12, 66, 69, 107

Uhud, Battle of 27
Umar bin al-Khattab 7, 15, 30, 38, 39,
    84, 92, 93, 95, 97, 100
umma (community) 8, 24, 31, 36, 37,
    57, 64, 73, 74––5, 111, 119
Umm Salama 39
Urban II, Pope 65
al-Uzza 10, 14, 34

veils 77, 86, 87, 95

Wansbrough, J. 100, 111
Watt, W. M. 8, 38, 100, 101, 102,
    105–7, 108, 120
women 51; and Quran (*Sharia*) 78–83;
    role of 77–97
world faiths 54–76

Yeats, W. B. 2

Zaynab bint Jahsh 84–5, 86, 89
Zoroastrians 62